SAP Enterprise Architecture

A Blueprint for Executing Digital Transformation

Sheunopa Chalmers Musukutwa

Apress®

SAP Enterprise Architecture: A Blueprint for Executing Digital Transformation

Sheunopa Chalmers Musukutwa
Johannesburg, South Africa

ISBN-13 (pbk): 978-1-4842-8574-9 ISBN-13 (electronic): 978-1-4842-8575-6
https://doi.org/10.1007/978-1-4842-8575-6

Copyright © 2022 by Sheunopa Chalmers Musukutwa

This work is subject to copyright. All rights are reserved by the Publisher, whether the whole or part of the material is concerned, specifically the rights of translation, reprinting, reuse of illustrations, recitation, broadcasting, reproduction on microfilms or in any other physical way, and transmission or information storage and retrieval, electronic adaptation, computer software, or by similar or dissimilar methodology now known or hereafter developed.

Trademarked names, logos, and images may appear in this book. Rather than use a trademark symbol with every occurrence of a trademarked name, logo, or image we use the names, logos, and images only in an editorial fashion and to the benefit of the trademark owner, with no intention of infringement of the trademark.

The use in this publication of trade names, trademarks, service marks, and similar terms, even if they are not identified as such, is not to be taken as an expression of opinion as to whether or not they are subject to proprietary rights.

While the advice and information in this book are believed to be true and accurate at the date of publication, neither the authors nor the editors nor the publisher can accept any legal responsibility for any errors or omissions that may be made. The publisher makes no warranty, express or implied, with respect to the material contained herein.

Managing Director, Apress Media LLC: Welmoed Spahr
Acquisitions Editor: Divya Modi
Development Editor: Laura Berendson
Coordinating Editor: Divya Modi

Cover designed by eStudioCalamar

Cover image designed by Pixabay

Distributed to the book trade worldwide by Springer Science+Business Media New York, 1 New York Plaza, Suite 4600, New York, NY 10004-1562, USA. Phone 1-800-SPRINGER, fax (201) 348-4505, e-mail orders-ny@springer-sbm.com, or visit www.springeronline.com. Apress Media, LLC is a California LLC and the sole member (owner) is Springer Science + Business Media Finance Inc (SSBM Finance Inc). SSBM Finance Inc is a **Delaware** corporation.

For information on translations, please e-mail booktranslations@springernature.com; for reprint, paperback, or audio rights, please e-mail bookpermissions@springernature.com.

Apress titles may be purchased in bulk for academic, corporate, or promotional use. eBook versions and licenses are also available for most titles. For more information, reference our Print and eBook Bulk Sales web page at http://www.apress.com/bulk-sales.

Any source code or other supplementary material referenced by the author in this book is available to readers on GitHub via the book's product page, located at www.apress.com/. For more detailed information, please visit http://www.apress.com/source-code.

Printed on acid-free paper

This book is dedicated to the Musukutwa Clan and especially dedicated to Judith, Sheanesu, Jeremy, Annan and Aretha.

Table of Contents

About the Author

 **Sheunopa Chalmers Musukutwa** is a seasoned SAP Consultant and Technical Business Analyst who began his career over a decade ago. He was part of a team that carried out the first implementation of SAP Business Suite on HANA in Africa. Starting out as an SAP Technical Consultant, Sheunopa transitioned into an SAP Business Intelligence Consultant and Business Analyst. This broadened his horizons and allowed him to understand SAP from a holistic perspective. His technical background allows him to translate the use and benefits of technology to business people. Sheunopa possesses multiple SAP certifications and is a graduate of the University of South Africa.

About the Technical Reviewer

 **Ishmael Makitla** has a rare combination of scientific and academic rigor, strong technical expertise, and an uncommon tolerance for difficult tasks all of which have seen him succeed in all environments where he applied his trade. His background covers scientific and industrial research, academia, and FinTech (specifically the banking domain). Ishmael joined a large Sandton-based investment bank as a Senior FinTech Developer (Java) and later became a DevOps Lead, responsible for software development and environment management. In the few years that he's been with the bank, he has contributed significantly to the marked improvement in the stability and performance of the statutory and regulatory reporting and data analytics platform. He also worked on the Corporate Cash Manager platform for one of the private banks where he was responsible for the implementation of an enhanced and automated AML screening for client onboarding. Before moving into the banking domain, Ishmael was a Senior Technologist at the Council for Scientific and Industrial Research (CSIR) for eight years (2009–2017). During this time, he worked on various complex projects, including the Health Population Registration System for which he built the data synchronization system. Ishmael won multiple awards for his contributions and was also awarded four Technology Demonstrators/ Inventions while at CSIR, bearing testament to the depth of his technical knowledge and scientific understanding. He is currently writing his doctoral thesis as a Doctoral Candidate at the University of South Africa

(UNISA) studying toward a Ph.D. in Computer Science; he holds a master's degree (Cum Laude) in Information Technology from Nelson Mandela Metropolitan University (2012). He also holds a bachelor's degree in technology (B.Tech.) in Engineering Computer Systems from Tshwane University of Technology (2008). His Ph.D. study focuses on developing a collaborative and corroborative Semantic Web Service Monitoring mechanism. He is currently exploring topics such as philosophy of technology, future Internet applications, enterprise architecture, platform-based business models, semantic data mining, and ontology engineering as well as emerging FinTechs and DevOps. He has co-authored academic conference papers and made presentations at conferences and workshops; he has been invited to give talks at conferences and on public media (TV/radio stations). His previous involvements in the academic and tech communities include Eskom Expo for Young Scientists International Science Fair, Country Mentor for Google Developer Groups, Random Hacks of Kindness (RHoK) Pretoria Chapter, part-time lecturer (for B.Tech.), reviewing for online tech courses (Udacity: Android), conferences, and journal articles.

Acknowledgments

Divya Modi and the Apress team have worked tirelessly to ensure that the book is well written, structured, and completed on time. The impact of their efforts on the writing of this book has been invaluable, and I am truly thankful.

I would like to extend my deepest gratitude to Ishmael Makitla who has ensured that this book is technically sound through his thorough and in-depth technical reviews of every chapter. In the same vein, I would like to thank Sijabuliso Nkiwane for putting me in touch with Ishmael. Ishmael has offered his valuable practical experience in the area of Enterprise Architecture to steer this book in the desired direction.

Introduction

What is enterprise architecture?

Ask ten different people and get ten different answers. Every business has an architecture, whether it is aware of it or not. Every business consists of elements that make it tick. Business goals and objectives, various stakeholders, data, applications, servers, disaster recovery sites, and the list goes on and on. How does your business manage all of these elements? Furthermore, how does your business manage these elements in a way that leads to strategic advantage?

Enterprise architecture may mean different things to different people, but one thing we cannot disagree on is its importance. It is quite literally a means to not only surviving but thriving in a constantly changing world. Years ago, an ERP project could stretch from three to five years, which is far from today's reality. Organizations are expected to be agile and adapt to the conditions of their environment at a moment's notice. The number one question is "how?" This book serves as the answer to that question in an SAP context, though the principles in this book can be applied to any business.

The answer to the question "how?" starts by establishing where your business is now. Enterprise Architecture is about vividly describing where your business is today through modelling the processes, capabilities, resources, data, and technological assets that sustain your business in a way understood by multiple stakeholders. This is achieved through the multiperspective approach that Enterprise Architecture provides. This process is extended to capturing the vision of the future of the business, once again, through modelling the aforementioned elements. Enterprise Architecture also allows for the modelling of intermediary states between the current and future states of your business.

This book provides a practical look at how to go about using SAP Enterprise Architecture Designer to model and document your Enterprise Architecture. However, a holistic approach has been taken in the writing of this book through starting with the very basics of Enterprise Architecture. This means that this book is suitable for people that are new to Enterprise Architecture all the way to advanced readers who are looking to apply this knowledge in the real world.

Ultimately, Enterprise Architecture provides a solid base for planning, analysis, decision making, and strategy execution. It is similar to a puzzle in which you initially figure out what pieces are currently at your disposal and how they fit together; thereafter, you decide what pieces are missing to complete the puzzle you envision; then you set about creating those pieces. This is the essence of enterprise architecture and what separates it from merely developing systems; the enterprise is the system!

Elements such as the individual systems, processes, capabilities, and data within your business are pieces to a puzzle; Enterprise Architecture is how you piece that puzzle together.

CHAPTER 1

Introducing Enterprise Architecture

The business ecosystem has become more and more complicated over time. Over the years, change has continued to be a constant, and businesses have increased in agility in order to better equip themselves for survival. Change in the business environment has generally come in the following forms:

- Technological change that has revolutionized operations and introduced new business models

- Increased competition from start-ups and legacy companies alike

- Greater customer expectations

- Changes in regulatory landscape

These factors have created complexity in the business ecosystem that must be navigated accordingly. For instance, there is no way your business can be certain how regulations may change in the next five years, but your business can make decisions today that will ensure that it will be flexible and agile enough to navigate those changes. Maintaining the ability to

© Sheunopa Chalmers Musukutwa 2022
S. C. Musukutwa, *SAP Enterprise Architecture*, https://doi.org/10.1007/978-1-4842-8575-6_1

adapt to new business demands will not only ensure an enterprise's survival but can ultimately lead to a competitive advantage.

As mentioned, there is no way to predict most of the changes an enterprise will encounter; however, Enterprise Architecture enables your business to be agile enough to adapt to a changing environment. From the onset, building the right technological infrastructure to support an enterprise's business needs is crucial. Consider the following scenario.

Your business may purchase software to address a specific need at a particular point in time. Over time, business needs will change. Your business should be flexible enough to change in accordance with new business needs, which may mean replacing that software. This transition should occur without significantly affecting the existing Enterprise Architecture if the enterprise's business processes have been designed to be solution-agnostic. Unfortunately, if the architecture that was used to select that software was lacking or nonexistent, it's likely going to be a difficult process filled with patch work. This is the fundamental issue with legacy systems.

In the 1960s, intentional information systems planning was introduced to incorporate strategy into the design of information systems and has since evolved to address different challenges. One particular challenge presented itself in the 1990s. At the time, siloed IT systems meant that integration and interoperability were major issues. Businesses wanted their systems to cut across these silos, share information, and achieve holistic integration. Information systems planning facilitated this by considering end-to-end data flows between departments and determining management information requirements in the context of the entire business. Solution architects began to adopt a structured approach to design solutions that accommodated growth and innovation in order to address changing business needs.

Over time, the same approach of building an IT landscape equipped for change has been expanded to the entire enterprise. With the rise in adoption of middleware and Service-Oriented Architecture putting an end to siloed IT systems, the focus changed to the business and IT alignment, enabling the businesses as a whole to adapt to change in a coherent manner. Information technology can now be classified as a change enabler by being flexible enough to offer the capabilities required by changing business needs. The concept of Enterprise Architecture has developed into a multiperspective view of business processes, business objectives, data, systems, and IT infrastructure.

Enterprise Architecture is a globally recognized discipline with its own standards, frameworks, and best practices. It is important to note that even though a business may not specifically utilize EA to build their business, the business will still have an architecture, whether it has been consciously designed or not. As we shall explore in this book, an enterprise's architecture consists of components such as its people, technology, and business capabilities within the context of how they relate to each other in attaining strategic goals.

In summary, EA involves

- Insight into the components that form your enterprise and the relationships between these components

- Articulating an enterprise's desired future state to drive your enterprise's business strategy

- Defining steps, standards, and guidelines required to transition toward a desired future state of your enterprise

- A basis for the control, overseeing, and management of change

- Providing a reliable reference to support management decision making

An agile Enterprise Architecture allows businesses to apply changes to processes and capabilities rapidly. The right architecture defines the present and desired future states of an enterprise while facilitating the transition to that future state. This book will explore what Enterprise Architecture is, its value, and its application to equip you with the knowledge to navigate business change and complexity. The book starts off by laying a standard foundation of Enterprise Architecture (EA) before focusing on SAP Enterprise Architecture and SAP Enterprise Architecture Designer specifically.

EA has evolved from only consisting of technological systems but now includes the goals, makeup, and running of your business. The next section seeks to further articulate the definition of EA.

Defining Enterprise Architecture

If you ask ten people what Enterprise Architecture is, you're sure to get ten different answers. This is largely because EA can be defined differently depending on the context in which it is being utilized. For instance, for an organization seeking to align its IT capabilities with its business goals:

> *Enterprise architecture is the process by which an organization standardizes and organizes IT infrastructure to align with its business vision and strategic goals.*

The following would be a definition suited to an enterprise looking to utilize EA to navigate business change and complexity:

> *Enterprise architecture is a process of consciously leading how an enterprise adapts to change by conceptualizing and overseeing the transition toward a desired future business state.*

Both definitions encompass what EA is in the sense that it establishes the current state (as-is) of an organization while articulating a future desired state (to-be). These two states are used to identify the gap between where your enterprise is and where you want it to be in the future. Your enterprise can now formulate the measures required to fill that gap and to embark on the transition to a future state; this is where the alignment of IT capabilities and business requirements transpires (see Figure 1-1).

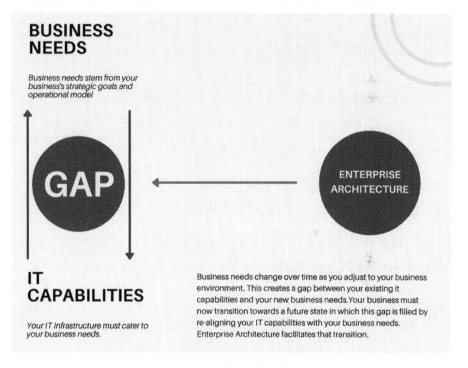

Figure 1-1. *Aligning IT capabilities to business needs*

Building a physical structure is similar to building an enterprise. Building any kind of physical structure without a blueprint will likely lead to the wrong result and wasteful expenditure. Enterprise Architecture acts as a blueprint that offers a clear direction and reference point that allows you to manage your enterprise and its resources effectively.

Enterprise Architecture allows a business to realize multiple benefits such as

- Clarity to understand relationships between organizational components

- Agility to adapt to change

- Foresight to recognize opportunities

- A road map to facilitate the transition to a desired future step

- Improved planning, decision-making, and solution implementation

EA has multiple definitions because businesses utilize it with different end goals in mind and experience different benefits from it. Each organization will define EA according to what they hope to achieve by utilizing it. The key to understanding EA across multiple contexts is by defining the words that make up EA, "Enterprise" and "Architecture."

What Is an Enterprise?

Simply put, an enterprise is any human endeavor – people collaborating together for a common purpose, supported by a platform. These people may be organized as a company or a project team. The supporting platform may include buildings, equipment, and information technology. Through the sharing of information, an enterprise performs related and collaborative activities toward achieving a common goal. The word enterprise generally gives the idea that we are referring to large corporate organizations, which is not always the case as an enterprise can be an organization of any size. Private companies, government agencies, nonprofit organizations, or a business unit within a large organization can be seen as an enterprise. This is because even an individual business unit has its own goals, business processes, skills and resources, and IT capabilities that support it.

An enterprise consists of multiple components that must all be taken into consideration within the context of the enterprise's strategic goals. Achieving this requires the design of a balanced and integrated enterprise built upon the conscious decisions of its leaders. An enterprise depends on the optimal collaboration of its people, their competencies, business processes, IT, products and services, and its environment to meet business goals. This is the point at which we begin to see a structure forming.

What Is an Architecture?

An architecture is comprised of models and visual descriptions that represent the structure of an enterprise. In short, just as an architect builds a house according to a blueprint, an architect is required to build an enterprise according to a set of specifications that will result in achieving the business vision. Some confusion may arise around the fact that architecture is both the act and the result of analysis, design, and implementation. In the context of EA, analysis, documentation, and modelling are all processes within architecture, while the end product, "an architecture," is the depiction of the composition and processes of the enterprise.

As mentioned in the introduction, the architecture of an enterprise exists whether or not it is acknowledged by the enterprise. Enterprises consist of processes, employees, locations, data, applications, and technology. The structure and the arrangement of all these components is the architecture of the enterprise. All of these components will interact in some way to create a structure that ultimately becomes your enterprise's architecture. EA allows this to become a conscious process, one managed according to specific frameworks, standards, and best practices. The "enterprise" view is strategic and encompasses your whole organization, while its "architecture" provides a formal and best practice approach to building the enterprise.

The combination of the two words, "Enterprise" and "Architecture," produces a clearer picture.

The Big Picture

Enterprise architecture offers a blueprint of the enterprise on a holistic level, and it becomes clear that seemingly independent components are actually interdependent. This is contrary to the modular or system-centric approaches utilized in past analysis techniques. It is a way of thinking about the structure of an enterprise that provides a specific approach of describing and understanding the structure of an enterprise. The end result is an enterprise-wide view of the enterprise structure which in turn exposes the limitations and constraints of the enterprise. This big picture view of an enterprise is what positions EA as an instrument to articulate the future while being the plan of transition toward that same future.

A blueprint that articulates how your enterprise utilizes IT resources and capabilities in reaching its strategic goals is a crucial point of departure. Every business has goals it wishes to achieve and a way it wishes to operate. This in turn creates business needs that must be met for the business to operate toward meeting its strategic goals. IT plays a crucial role in meeting business needs while also being an enabler for change. A business's strategic goals and operating model have to be aligned with its IT capabilities and infrastructure.

The ongoing management activities of planning, organizing, leading, and controlling are required to support the establishment of an Enterprise Architecture through the deployment of formal, standardized processes. This management program should be a part of an enterprise's more common management practices such as risk management or strategic planning; see Figure 1-2. This establishes EA as a business-as-usual activity and further entrenches it as a cornerstone for business success. Managing EA is made exponentially easier when there is one big picture the enterprise is working toward.

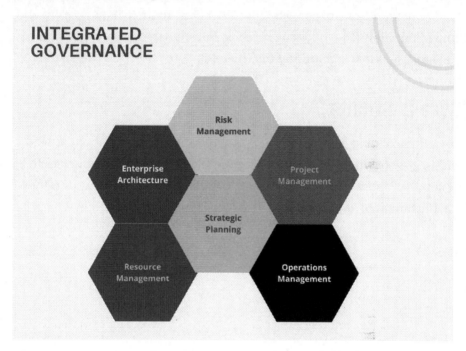

Figure 1-2. *Integrated governance*

Figure 1-2 displays common management practices undertaken by a business. EA should ideally be implemented as a management practice backed by executive endorsement. As EA is an enterprise-wide endeavor, it takes all other management practices into account when articulating the state of the business.

The big picture of EA should serve as a reference point, both as a plan and a map – as a plan in the sense that it captures the enterprise's design, processes, and goals and as a map by providing the direction, next steps, standards, and best practices to be followed in going about bringing the enterprise to life. A single reference such as this eliminates the chances for the duplication of work as it is clear who is who and what is what in the grand scheme of things. The enterprise establishes a state of synergy and progresses in unison.

EA includes several core elements that contribute to its successful implementation. The following sections introduce these core elements that are also unpacked throughout the book.

Core Elements

Regardless of the approach being taken to establish the EA practice within your business, there are several core elements that are integral to its success. These core elements seek to guide, manage, and support the establishment of an EA practice. The core elements are as follows:

> EA framework
>
> EA methodology
>
> Current architecture
>
> Future architecture
>
> EA management plan
>
> EA artifacts
>
> Best practices

The following sections will introduce each of these elements to provide an idea of what EA comprises.

EA Framework

An Enterprise Architecture framework is a description of how to develop and utilize an Enterprise Architecture. An Enterprise Architecture Framework is comprised of standards, practices, templates, and guidelines to be followed in producing and utilizing the resultant Enterprise Architecture. It structures the thinking of the architectural team by dividing the Enterprise Architecture into domains. It determines the breadth of the complete architecture and how the various sub-architecture levels relate.

It assists architects to understand how a business's systems and assets are logically structured and connected. This in turn supports holistic design decisions on all the domains of the architecture.

The specific manner in which the EA Framework distinguishes, collects, and organizes the domains results in a conceptual collection of "views" of an enterprise. This is particularly handy in the case of large and complex enterprises as the benefits of framework adoption typically become more apparent as the complexity and diversity of the architecture increases. EA frameworks are important tools for enterprises that are undergoing digital transformation initiatives. Enterprise modelling software tools such as SAP Enterprise Architecture Designer can make implementation and management of a framework easier.

The elements of your EA Framework provide a sense of direction that is split into three areas:

Architecture description – This defines the documentation process of your enterprise from multiple viewpoints. The point of the different viewpoints is to accommodate all stakeholders and also to ensure that the possible effects of any decision can be considered from every angle. To successfully implement an Enterprise Architecture framework, each enterprise stakeholder should be able to understand the architecture from their own viewpoint within the organization.

Design method – This describes the processes that enterprise architects must adopt to model the Enterprise Architecture. This may be broken down into phases with each process having its goals, inputs, stages, and outputs.

Team structure – This is a guideline on how the team of your enterprise architects must be structured and governed. It further details the level of competency, experience, and training needed. The framework should document skills gaps so training can be conducted.

Ultimately, an EA Framework serves as the perfect starting point by providing tools, techniques, and procedures that equip enterprise architects to get the most out of different architecture domains and integrate processes to create an agile environment that can undergo change while still meeting strategic goals.

EA is typically divided into four domains:

- Business Architecture

- Application Architecture

- Data Architecture

- Infrastructure Architecture

See Figure 1-3. Please note that the naming conventions of these domains may differ according to the EA framework being utilized.

Business Architecture

Business architecture captures how a business operates and communicates how IT supports the business. It aligns technology strategy to business strategy, business capabilities, and value chains. The business architecture can be used to develop business/technology road maps, design future technology architecture to adapt to change, or design operating models. Business Architecture articulates the reason the organization exists and includes its objectives, goals, strategic thinking, capabilities, and organizational structure.

Application Architecture

Application Architecture provides fit-for-purpose and easy-to-use applications to support the business operations detailed in the business architecture. It primarily deals with user interfaces, integrations, and workflows. What is key is the data consumed and produced by applications rather than their internal structure. An application architecture details the functionality of applications utilized in your business and how they relate.

Data Architecture

Applications need data to work, and the data architecture connects enterprise data and makes it consumable. Data Architecture includes rules, standards, policies, and models that determine the nature of the data to be collected, the manner in which it is stored and leveraged by your business. A data architecture describes the data structure utilized by your business applications and business processes.

NB* You may find that some EA frameworks have the data and application domain as one combined information system layer. This book details each domain separately in an aim to provide a more precise and granular description of the domains.

Infrastructure Architecture

This refers to the underlying infrastructure required to run the business – the nuts and bolts, so to speak. It describes the logical software and hardware capabilities that are required to support the deployment of business, data, and application services. The type of network topology, servers, client computers, IOT devices, and databases must be considered in relation to the objectives of the business architecture.

EA offers a comprehensive view of all these four domains, and after this brief overview, it should be clear how the coordination of these four domains results in IT and business alignment. Each domain has its own goals, objectives, standards, and processes, but they must all work toward achieving the enterprise's strategic goals.

Additional Domains

As EA has grown as a discipline, different frameworks have been developed that include additional domains beyond the core domains mentioned thus far. One of particular interest is the security architecture because of more people working from home, the proliferation of the Internet of Things devices, and the increase in cybersecurity threats.

Security Architecture

As depicted in Figure 1-3, the security domain cuts through all the abovementioned domains dealing with how your business secures the artifacts within it and how it mitigates the risks it faces. Security architecture has traditionally consisted of predictive, preventive, detective, and corrective measures deployed to safeguard the enterprise's digital assets. However, this also includes establishing the organization's security posture by providing adequate cybersecurity education and training throughout the enterprise.

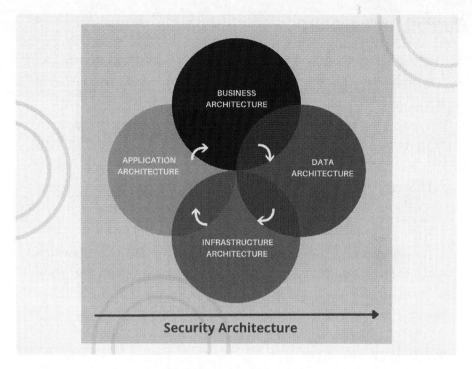

Figure 1-3. *Enterprise Architecture domains*

Demarcating the enterprise into different domains reduces the complexity of dealing with large enterprises especially.

EA Methodology

A methodology is a structured and systematic collection of approaches used to establish and maintain the Enterprise Architecture program. A methodology explicitly directs an architect's thinking toward the desired outcome along with supporting why that line of thought should be taken. It tells us what steps to take, in what order, and how to perform those steps.

Current Architecture

The current-state architecture represents where the organization is today and possibly how it got there. This is commonly referred to as the "as-is" view. It gives insight into the resources, processes, activities, skillsets, charts, diagrams, manuals, goals, and objectives (among other artifacts) that the enterprise currently has. These items are referred to as artifacts in the EA context. At a granular level, there is a view of this for a particular line of business or segment. The current architecture must be analyzed, designed, and documented in the same manner as the future architecture so that gaps in performance between the two can be clearly seen.

An accurate picture of the current architecture is critical because it forms the basis of project planning and investment decision making. When used in combination with the future architecture, it's easier to evaluate existing architecture against long-term goals.

Future Architecture

The future architecture is a vision of how your business intends on leveraging its IT capabilities to support business operations at a specific time in the future.

It details the new artifacts that will be required to achieve one of the following:

- Business objectives

- Optimize performance by closing an existing performance gap and achieving operational targets

- Support business strategies (new and existing)

- Support operational requirements (new and existing)

- Digital transformation

This process of articulating the future must be coordinated and make strategic (business direction), tactical (business processes), and operational (technology) considerations that will result in the achievement of the new business goals.

In combination, the current and future architectures enable the development of a clear road map that will guide you in your transition from the current state to a future state. It is recommended that this road map include transient states to ensure that there are always tangible deliverables and goals to be met. Furthermore, this ensures that you stay on course and on time. Executing incrementally in accordance with predetermined checkpoints ensures that you are always aware of whether things are running efficiently or not. More importantly, you can tell whether the intended architecture is what you are actually likely to achieve.

The next step is to establish how the EA process will be governed. Clear and efficient governance procedures are critical in establishing the control required to guide the EA process toward desired outcomes.

EA Management Plan (EA Governance)

The EA management plan documents how EA will be governed and controlled. It translates the architectural requirements of your enterprise into digestible standards, actionable activities, and guidelines in the development of an Enterprise Architecture. Thus, the EA management plan serves as a reference document required to maintain a level of excellence in EA. For instance, the standards woven into the EA management plan include both business and technology standards that cover all domains of the EA. They include local standards, international standards, and industry standards. Internally, EA can be used to produce new standards for the enterprise.

17

The EA management plan may be broken down into corporate governance, IT governance, and architecture governance to contextualize governance procedures and their significance to the EA process. The EA management plan also contains information that supports EA management decision making such as an overview of the current and future state, the existing performance gaps, EA goals, available resources, and a sequencing plan.

The EA management plan is what they call a living document in the sense that it evolves over time and must continually be referenced. The EA management plan must be updated on predetermined dates or after important cycles or iterations to reflect accurate, relevant, and current information. Efficient version control of the EA management plan is crucial in ensuring that all stakeholders are on the same page. It is the focal point of utilizing EA in management.

Best Practices

These are procedures that have been proven effective in executing the discipline of Enterprise Architecture. They help manage Enterprise Architecture and have been established through trial and error. Following best practices results in business benefits such as more predictable outcomes. Examples are recommendations such as utilizing the business strategy as the starting point of EA or creating an EA charter. Best practices are expanded on in great length later in this book.

EA Artifacts

The core elements highlighted so far result in various models and documentation that represent the enterprise-wide big picture. It is important that all of these products are stored in a central location available to all relevant stakeholders to support the EA practice.

EA artifacts are documents that provide descriptions of the state of the enterprise and include documents such as business plans, workflows, network descriptions, and more in addition to the core elements that have been mentioned. They are cornerstones of an EA practice and improve the communication and collaboration between stakeholders. Artifacts are stored in what is called the EA repository. The EA repository is a central storage space for EA artifacts that various EA stakeholders can access.

To conclude the section on core elements, here is a summary of how all of these core elements come together.

The EA framework provides a structured approach to establishing the EA practice and guides the thinking adopted by the enterprise architects. It demarcates the enterprise as several domains typically including the Business Architecture, Data Architecture, Application Architecture, and Infrastructure Architecture. The EA methodology specifically details the activities and steps to be taken in each phase of the EA process along with the EA artifacts that must be produced in each phase.

The current architecture offers an "as-is" view that serves as the starting point for the enterprise's transition into a future state. The "to-be" view is articulated in terms of the future architecture. The gap analysis determines suitable options available to transition the business enterprise from the current to the future state while making the best use of available resources. The EA management plan provides continual governance through guiding the business in planning and controlling various EA activities. Best practices are tried and tested ways of carrying out EA activities that are likely to lead to desired outcomes if they are adopted effectively.

Thus far, this book has looked at EA as a practice. The following section expands on the role of an EA practitioner, in other words, an Enterprise Architect.

What Does an Enterprise Architect Do?

This chapter opened by highlighting the different ways EA can be defined based on the context in which it is being practiced. Naturally, this also leads to the role of an enterprise architect being ambiguous. Taking different perspectives and contexts into consideration, the following description encapsulates the role of an enterprise architect:

> *An enterprise architect ensures that a business leverages its resources, technologies and skills to reach its business outcomes by guiding and overseeing the business's transition to a desired future state.*

An enterprise architect provides strategic architecture vision and direction by leading architecture transformations and organizational change. For instance, after conducting a gap analysis, the enterprise architect must put together the migration plan to determine how these gaps will be filled. EA is not about executing the changes but about overseeing them. Enterprise architects do this by determining standards that must be followed by project teams. Enterprise architects must govern the change activities and ensure that the plan will actually achieve what the enterprise needs.

The duties of an enterprise architect include

- Ensuring IT capabilities match business needs

- Establishing architecture and process governance

- Communicating goals, metrics, and value across the organization

- Analyzing existing capabilities

- Establishing a road map to a future state

- Supporting planning and decision-making activities by providing analysis

- Defining the structure of the EA repository

An enterprise architect's goals would be as follows:

- Leverage technology to reduce manual processes and increase efficiency

- Better control costs within the organization, particularly technology and infrastructure

- Gain better control of data across the organization to eliminate redundancy and increase accuracy

- Increase competitive advantage and market share and increase customer base

Questions that an EA might have to tackle are as follows:

- Should the business utilize a cloud-based infrastructure?

- Should the business build, buy, or leverage managed services?

- Which system should the business migrate first?

- Does the business already have the technology to facilitate its goals or is an upgrade required?

The preceding goals, questions, and their answers must be linked to a plan of action that the enterprise architect is responsible for putting together. This plan has to be broken down into a phased approach that makes the best use of available resources. The output of an EA's work is the overall executive strategy into an implementable work plan.

An enterprise architect must always have an in-depth understanding of the environment they're working in order to plan the use of time, resources, and skills accordingly. This will further assist in managing the expectation of stakeholders because the enterprise architect has an understanding of what is possible and realistic. A wide range of experience and exposure to different technological solutions across multiple business departments enables the enterprise architect to maintain an enterprise-wide view.

Establishing an Effective EA Practice

The two previous sections introduced the EA process and the role of the enterprise architect. A firm understanding of the EA process, the enterprise architect, and the relationship between the two is necessary to establish a successful EA practice within your business. The factors key to establishing an effective EA practice can be summarized as follows:

1. Ensure the availability of competent resources to lead and govern architecture development within clearly defined roles and responsibilities.

2. Select a proven and agile implementation methodology that will be adhered to by the entire enterprise.

3. Best practices, standards, and guidelines must be readily available to all stakeholders, and there must be a system to monitor compliance.

4. Manage the EA repository effectively.

5. EA management should be part of an integrated governance model.

The Value of Enterprise Architecture

The value of Enterprise Architecture is seen from the perspective of the problems it addresses. Most of these problems stem from changes in the business environment. Most recently, the COVID-19 pandemic has sent shockwaves across the business world. Businesses that were already further along in their Enterprise Architecture journey were able to adapt rapidly after new complexities were introduced. With the growing work-from-anywhere culture, EA is no longer confined to the walls of corporate buildings. People, processes, and technologies meet business needs wherever business is done, which includes the home, the train, and coffee shop. Only agile organizations equipped for sudden change navigated these complexities successfully.

Enterprise Architecture allows the business to look at possible solutions and business requirements in the context of its strategic goals. We must always determine what we want to achieve first, then combine it with the relevant business processes and technology. This ensures that the business is considering the entire enterprise in its decision making and enables it to build an agile enterprise that can adapt rapidly in accordance with those decisions. Doing the reverse would result in a bottom-up, system-level approach which has historically been the cause of great financial loss as the enterprise continually changes its processes to accommodate legacy systems. System-level views may be sufficient for smaller organizations but are found wanting in the case of larger businesses.

EA is also valuable in terms of supporting management practices by providing insight into the enterprise at a holistic level. For example, it gives visibility into available resources and how they have been used. Decisions can then be made on how best to optimize those resources. This also forms the basis for the review of internal projects and initiatives. Management policies can be implemented upon the foundation of the insight provided by EA. The policies are built to support the transition to the desired future state as per the EA.

The value of Enterprise Architecture will be further expanded upon in the course of this book as more complex concepts become digestible.

Summary

This chapter served to provide a brief overview of EA suitable for readers from all backgrounds including readers new to EA. EA allows an organization to move in unison toward a shared business vision. It is a reference point that serves as a guide in how the organization should make decisions and manage processes in order to achieve its goals. Enterprise architecture is both a profession and a description of an expected result of practicing that profession.

EA has an enterprise-wide look of your systems that is within the context of your strategic goals. We can deduce what has to be done through analysis and design, how to do it (methodology/best practice), to what level it should be done (standards), and how to control the process (management program). An enterprise architect ensures that a company leverages its resources, technologies, and skills to reach its business outcomes by guiding and overseeing your enterprise's transition to a desired future state. They are responsible for documenting and overseeing the transition toward a desired future state.

In point form, EA is utilized for

- Alignment of IT capabilities and business needs

- Cost reduction in operational expenses

- Leveraging your enterprise's technology assets at the highest level

- Improving IT capabilities and capacity

- Integration of new technologies

- As a management program

- As a documentation program

The following chapters will expand on the ideas and concepts introduced in this chapter, with Chapter 2 expanding on the strategic role of Enterprise Architecture.

CHAPTER 2

Strategic Enterprise Architecture

Enterprise Architecture is by definition a business-driven endeavor that allows the business to identify and utilize the technology that best complements the operating model today and in the future. EA's main objective, which is also an advantage of EA, is enabling businesses to achieve strategic objectives through alignment of strategy and IT capabilities. This chapter aims to demonstrate how a clear and well-defined business strategy is the first step in achieving that alignment.

EA covers three fundamental questions:

- – What does your business want to do?

- – How does your business want to do it?

- – What technology is required to do it?

Your business strategy is the starting point of answering these questions.

Alignment

Alignment is a word you hear quite often in the world of technology, but what does it actually mean? The dictionary defines alignment as "arrangement in a straight line or in correct relative positions" or

© Sheunopa Chalmers Musukutwa 2022

S. C. Musukutwa, *SAP Enterprise Architecture*, https://doi.org/10.1007/978-1-4842-8575-6_2

"a position of agreement or alliance." Its vagueness, however, does not take away from its importance which can be seen in how the word has continued to be part of the technology nomenclature for over 30 years. Progressive organizations have always seen the value in blending efficient business management with IT capabilities for strategy execution.

Historically, achieving organizational alignment has proven somewhat elusive as evidenced by the continued mushrooming of IT silos as evidence. Achieving organizational alignment can lead to improved efficiency, cost savings, and gaining a strategic advantage. But what are we aligning? Referring to it as "organizational alignment" is still vague; more specifically, we are referring to the alignment of the business with its IT capabilities.

Enterprise Architecture has been a tool to utilize for custom development and not for businesses that were buying business application software. There was a greater emphasis on the "architecture" which included designing and documenting IT systems and not on optimizing both business and IT processes to generate value. Over the years, Enterprise Architecture has adopted a more holistic and strategy-driven approach that encourages the synergy of IT with business functions. The "architecture" became more about organizing the enterprise in a way that creates a foundation for strategy execution with Enterprise Architecture as the structural framework.

EA has often been seen as an overly complicated IT endeavor. This book seeks to demonstrate that it is, in fact, an organizational endeavor, top to bottom. In view of this, EA should be communicated and executed in a way that everyone in the organization can understand to achieve organizational alignment. The entire organization should understand where it is today, where it wants to be tomorrow, and how it will get there in unison. This is alignment. Alignment will allow the organization to leverage a long-term decision-making framework when multiple IT implementation options exist.

As this book has a focus on SAP applications, we will consider Enterprise Architecture in the context of packaged enterprise applications and how it helps to align business and IT. It is important for the business strategy to lead the EA endeavor because **what** (vision, objectives, goals) you are trying to achieve is what informs how you intend to achieve it (the operational model). The operational model describes the business processes within your business units, their level of standardization, distinguishing capabilities, integration, and the data they require. This in turn informs the design and implementation of the IT infrastructure required to support those business processes and therefore creates a foundation for business strategy execution. A formal introduction to SAP will be provided in Chapter 4.

EA can easily become a purely abstract exercise proliferated with esoteric terms that have no practical use. This book seeks to depart slightly from the old way of doing things by sticking to the basics. Success starts with building a master plan (a business strategy). We shall look at the components that make up that master plan, how they relate to each other, and ultimately how they support the capturing, describing, and governing of all IT capabilities across your organization in an effort to meet the strategic goals of the business.

EA is a continuous alignment process. It is continuous because the business environment constantly changes. It is a **Dynamic Alignment Process (DAP)**. An organization's business strategy forms the basis for this alignment, and it is crucial to understand the critical role of the business strategy in EA.

Understanding the Role of Business Strategy in Enterprise Architecture

Business strategy may be understood differently from one business to another; however, it can be generally understood as the objectives a business is pursuing and how they intend on attaining them.

Every enterprise has value-generating business functions that are supported by other functions. IT in itself does not create value but acts as a supporting function to the business functions. The enterprise architect must ensure that all investments in IT support the business functions adequately. Enterprise Architecture is the means through which an alignment of an enterprise's business strategy and IT strategy can be realized.

In its very nature, business strategy is a forward-looking, long-term endeavor. This makes it the perfect starting point for EA because it forms the foundation for producing EA artifacts that capture the future IT infrastructure required to support the business in executing that very strategy. This includes the basis for the articulation of a desired future state, that is, "the implementation of this strategy will have the organization in such and such a state in five years." Existing mainstream EA frameworks such as TOGAF version 9.2 generally recommend starting the EA effort from documenting the business strategy (goals, objectives, vision, etc.).

Developing EA from your business strategy provides much-needed context. Understanding what the business is trying to achieve on a strategic level is what allows you to determine the business processes that form part of the business capabilities. The execution of these business capabilities is critical to the business strategy. These business capabilities must be standardized and supported by the right (aligned) IT infrastructure to the greatest extent feasible. This alignment endeavor triggers a journey toward a desired future state in which the business capabilities are IT enabled, in other words, digital transformation. In this way, EA is informed by and also supports the execution of business strategy. Enterprise Architecture converts the business strategy into guiding principles that must be followed in digital transformation projects that implement change toward a desired future state.

The preceding process results in providing an aligned IT infrastructure for business execution, turning IT from a liability to an asset. The idea of Enterprise Architecture is to integrate business strategy, business capabilities, and IT capabilities in order to achieve a competitive advantage. A large part of this digital transformation involves automating the core capabilities. Automating these core capabilities allows the business to focus on the aspects of the business that cannot be automated because they are constantly changing. This puts the business in a position to be agile in regard to the more volatile aspects of the business while ensuring that the core capabilities are being delivered.

EA is a change enabler. This is important because business strategies generally change more frequently than the highly specific technologies used to support them, therefore creating the old age issue of legacy systems. EA allows you to work toward a future state while still being agile enough to accommodate change. When EA is executed accordingly, there is such a detailed understanding of the business that a complete overhaul is rarely ever required; areas in need of change can be isolated and transformed.

As mentioned, there is a real danger that EA can easily become a purely abstract, jargon-filled exercise. EA includes software applications, business processes, human resources, and IT infrastructure. Using the business strategy as a point of departure helps mitigate this trap of total abstraction as it minimizes the technical jargon and position IT in a way that business executives will understand. EA closes the communication gap between business and IT, facilitates information systems planning, and aids business and IT alignment.

With all that said, enterprise architects should still seek additional information about the enterprise beyond the business strategy. The decision to use the business strategy as a basis for Enterprise Architecture should be thoroughly evaluated. It should never be assumed that a business strategy is clear enough or understood well enough by the business to form a basis for Enterprise Architecture.

For instance, business strategy can only be fully evaluated within the context of business and IT capabilities.

29

Business Strategy, Business Capabilities, and IT Capabilities

A business IT infrastructure is the platform that supports the execution of its business strategy. In reality, most business strategies are not clear enough to use as a basis for decision making in regard to which technology to implement. For instance, the following may appear as goals of the business strategy:

- Increase customer satisfaction

- Diversify revenue streams

- Reduce production costs

- Reduce customer churn

These strategic goals are all very vague as a basis for IT infrastructure decision making because they're descriptive rather than prescriptive. For instance, we may assume that customer relationship management software might aid us in increasing customer satisfaction and reducing customer churn, but how do we know the right CRM for our enterprise? We must have insight into the existing business processes that address customer relationship management and how IT can support them to achieve the stated goals. It is also possible that there may be a need to develop new IT-enabled business processes. In either case, the enterprise's business capabilities must be articulated because it is these business capabilities that can be aligned with IT on a more detailed level.

Business Capabilities

Business capabilities depict the required business process integration, standardization, and data for the enterprise to meet its daily mandate; see Figure 2-1. An enterprise's business capabilities provide a more practical view of the enterprise than its business strategy and form a better foundation for alignment. Business and IT alignment ceases to be a generic process but one that is tailored to the specific business. For instance, several companies may share the same goal of increasing revenue, but each company will go about it according to its own unique business capabilities. Therefore, alignment must take place between the business capabilities and the IT capabilities.

IT Capabilities

IT capabilities refer to how well IT supports business process needs through the deployment, maintenance, and support of IT solutions in a cost-effective manner under a robust governance framework. Accordingly, IT executives work to align IT capabilities with business capabilities by approving and implementing the technology recommended by the Enterprise Architect.

The best way to implement the process of alignment is to see IT as a service provider to the enterprise who serves the enterprise's business capability needs. Broadly speaking, the services IT provides include IT-enabled business process improvement, operational excellence (email, help desk support, server maintenance, etc.), and innovation which may lead to repositioning the business in the market.

In Figure 2-1, we see that within business capabilities are core capabilities that must be prioritized because they have the potential to distinguish the enterprise from its competitors and result in a competitive advantage.

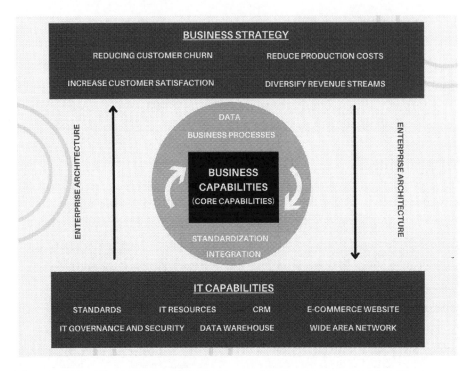

Figure 2-1. *The relationship between business strategy, business capabilities, and IT capabilities*

Core capabilities are the business capabilities that generate the most value within your business. They are identified by the value they bring to the enterprise and mapped to the relevant information technology that supports them. This mapping process enables the identification of the information technology services that are currently not available to the core capability but represent untapped potential and room for improvement.

Let us consider a business that has product development as one of its core capabilities. Your enterprise may have set the strategic goal to introduce new and innovative products to the market. One of the crucial factors in this process is speed to market. The product development team will need a reliable and fast Internet connection to access insights from information markets and to facilitate efficient communication via email, online meeting platforms, or VOIP. These basic services may seem insignificant, but they support important aspects of new product development such as making the go/no-go decision about a new concept. The quicker an informed decision can be made, the quicker a product can go to market. The performance of this strategic initiative will then be measured according to the revenue generated from the new products.

Through interrogating the business strategy (strategic goals specifically) and conversations with the product development team in business terms they can understand, the Enterprise Architect and IT executives identify the preceding scenario as a key area for IT investment and begin the process of translating business objectives into measurable IT services:

1. Analysis of the product development core capability

2. Recommend the technology, IT resources, and IT-enabled processes required to address the needs of the product development core capability

3. Scope and lead the project to implement change

In conclusion, as much as business strategy is a great starting point for EA, it is not the best basis on which to build alignment with IT (capabilities). In most cases, it is vague, and, secondly, strategic initiatives tend to change faster than the IT infrastructure that supports them as enterprises listen to their customers, counteract competitor initiatives, or capitalize on new opportunities. Whereas the business strategy ensures that EA is always considered in the context of a long-term vision, the business capabilities ensure that EA remains cognizant of what must take place on a day-to-day basis to achieve that vision.

There are two key questions that must be addressed at the beginning of the EA journey in regard to business strategy:

1. Is there a clearly defined and recognized business strategy?

2. Does it provide a clear and actionable direction?

The answers to these questions are important because they determine whether the EA endeavor can be contextualized. If the answer is no, a clear and actionable business strategy must first be documented and form the point of departure. The business strategy influences the scope of the EA endeavor and the basis for monitoring it against set goals. Furthermore, the business strategy can be used to establish synergy between all stakeholders on an enterprise-wide level despite their individual interests.

Enterprise Architecture can be best understood as a journey with a starting point and a set direction toward a destination. The following points summarize the main aspects of what has been discussed thus far:

- The business strategy is the starting point as well as the foundation of envisioning a desired future state (where we are and where we intend to travel to).

- Business capabilities articulate the business strategy in terms of what must be done to execute the business strategy (how we will travel).

- IT capabilities are the platform for the execution of the business capabilities and the business strategy (the fuel and supplies for our travel).

The preceding points highlight the relationship between business strategy, business capabilities, and IT capabilities. It is important for this relationship to be as coherent and streamlined as possible to ultimately achieve the goals set out in the business strategy. The required level of efficiency can only be realized through the alignment of the business capabilities and IT capabilities. The next section looks at the role the enterprise architect must play in achieving this alignment.

The Role of the Enterprise Architect in IT and Business Alignment

Generally, management starts by creating a business strategy. Ideally, IT and business collaborate to design IT-enabled solutions to achieve the goals of said business strategy. IT then builds the IT infrastructure to support the solutions. These IT-enabled solutions go live, and IT proceeds to manage the infrastructure while offering support to business. This seems simple enough, but there are stumbling blocks that enterprises have faced over the years. The primary one is a disconnect between business and IT. Does business language or IT jargon take precedence?

Achieving IT and business alignment becomes easier when the entire enterprise speaks a common language. Often, the same word can mean different things; EA's multidomain approach (business, data, application, and infrastructure domains) translates the relationships between domains into a common language. EA documents IT and business processes in a way the applicable stakeholders understand.

In order to leverage Enterprise Architecture as a strategic tool, the Enterprise Architect must engage closely with business leadership, subject matter experts, and other stakeholders on their terms. It is the enterprise architect's job to understand the enterprise's strategic goals and business needs. An enterprise architect must take part in the enterprise's business strategy planning meetings as it is crucial for the enterprise architect to engage business leaders on the business strategy. The business leaders can explain how they understand it and what they hope to achieve from it in detail.

The enterprise architect must also be able to understand business issues and maintain an ongoing dialogue to clarify business needs in business terms. This is important for two reasons:

1. Understanding the enterprise's business issues and business priorities allows for the effective allocation of IT resources to maximize business value. The enterprise architect must always keep in mind that Enterprise Architecture is a means for IT value creation.

2. Having a continual dialogue with business leaders allows the enterprise architect to anticipate and plan for any required changes in IT services to adapt to changes in the business environment, therefore being proactive rather than reactive.

Figure 2-2 depicts the possible questions an enterprise architect may ask when executing their duties.

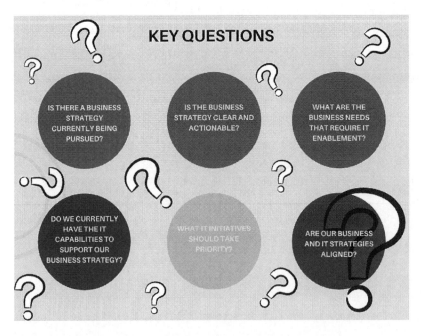

Figure 2-2. *Key questions an enterprise architect asks*

The short and precise key questions in Figure 2-2 trigger discussions that allow the enterprise architect to have an understanding of the current relationship between business and IT. The answers to these questions can provide an early indication of problem areas, for example, the absence of a clear business strategy or the lack of understanding/knowledge of the business strategy.

In view of the preceding questions in Figure 2-2, a substantial amount of information will come from having conversations with various stakeholders whether the enterprise architect is asking the questions or providing the answers. It should be clear that the key factor in the success of an Enterprise Architect's role is verbal and written communication. For instance, one of the main roles of an enterprise architect is to articulate how required technical changes will generate business value. This is done by showing the dollar value of the losses caused by the current technology systems or by demonstrating the monetary value of the proposed technical initiative. From the perspective of DevOps, the enterprise architect must encourage an environment that allows for the close collaboration of development teams and business functions in fostering IT and business alignment.

In the context of IT and business alignment, the enterprise architect's responsibilities are as follows:

- Engaging stakeholders to understand business strategy, budgets, opportunities, and threats. (One of the stumbling blocks of EA is managing multiple expectations from different stakeholders. The only way to get past this is to understand what is good for the business above and beyond everything else.)

- Creating a strategic plan describing the areas for improvement, untapped potential, and the gaps between IT and business.

–   Working with IT and business to formulate and document policies, standards, guidelines, and procedures that align IT services with business requirements.

–   Proposing technical solutions that best align with business capabilities.

–   Monitoring progress and taking corrective action.

How to Approach IT and Business Alignment

There are numerous ways to approach IT and business alignment, but they all generally involve a combination of plan, design, and manage:

1. **Plan**

    This first stage involves understanding the business objectives and capabilities well enough to determine the IT services that can support them in creating maximum business value. Services should not be implemented because they are an industry standard but because there is a good business case demonstrating a clear return on investment. It is crucial to gain an understanding of the business objectives in terms that the enterprise architect and the business leaders understand. This is also the time to come up with the governance structure, service-level agreements, and performance metrics that will be used to manage the IT services. The planning stage is essentially continuous because an open dialogue must be maintained to accommodate changes in business needs in the future. It is important to prioritize the business objectives and capabilities according to the business value the enterprise expects to derive from them as this will form the basis of how the business prioritizes IT resources. This forms a priority hierarchy based on business impact. Trade-off analyses take place to determine what IT services will be essential and which ones will be "nice-to-haves."

2. **Design**

    This is when we model the IT infrastructure required to deliver the IT services identified in the planning phase. This includes the resources, IT processes, IT assets, and skills that will be leveraged in delivering the IT services. Each of these components must be mapped back to the IT service they support and associated with specific standards and service levels.

3. **Manage**

    Once the IT infrastructure has gone live, it begins to support the relevant business capabilities. It is important for the IT team to have a robust and central management tool to respond to support requests from business. Support requests must be prioritized in terms of the business impact hierarchy established in the planning stage. A change management procedure will be required to ensure that all change requests are adequately considered, and informed decisions are taken to action on them or otherwise.

    – The monitoring of the delivery of IT services and performance of IT capabilities is a critical one. The performance metrics of software, IT processes, and IT resources have historically been considered in isolation without an enterprise view of their impact. However, metrics and analytics must be interpreted within a business context and with the consideration of the business impact hierarchy to address issues with the relevant urgency. The EA process can help in identifying the need for standards, frameworks, and best practices relevant to managing the IT environment such as the Information Technology Infrastructure Library (ITIL).

Typical Alignment Scenarios

As mentioned in the section "Alignment," the initial step in determining how to align is the business strategy. Understanding the enterprise's goals, objectives as per the business strategy will allow the enterprise architect to determine what business capabilities take priority in achieving them and what IT infrastructure will support them adequately. Table 2-1 shows some examples of how business agility, business standardization, and business strategy typically differ between organizations in relation to their size.

Table 2-1. *Examples of Business Agility, Standardization, and Strategy According to Enterprise Size*

Type of Enterprise	Business Agility	Business Standardization	Business Strategy
Small enterprise	High	Low	Differentiation
Medium enterprise	Medium	Medium	Balance of the two
Large enterprise	Low	High	Cost leadership

Business agility, business standardization, and business strategy influence how IT alignment can take place for each organization. The following subsections elaborate on these contextual differences:

Small enterprise (row 2)

Business agility: High

Business standardization: Low

Business strategy: Differentiation

Small enterprises typically take on a differentiation strategy by rapid product development and high responsiveness to customer needs to deliver bespoke services. In an effort to enhance business agility, there is minimal bureaucracy and standardization in order to foster speedy innovation. Staff are likely to utilize the applications that they believe best support their function sometimes even without the knowledge of IT. This is referred to as Shadow IT. The core IT services such as email and Internet connection remain standardized. As a result, an enterprise architect will focus mostly on the components of IT infrastructure that can be standardized to support the business functions without taking away from the small enterprise's agility.

Medium enterprise (row 3)

Business agility: Medium

Business standardization: Medium

Business strategy: Balance of differentiation and cost leadership

Medium enterprises have the opportunity to take on a balance of both differentiation and cost leadership strategy. In this case, the enterprise architect may seek to standardize the IT capabilities that support business functions such as finance or HR while maintaining more agile IT capabilities to support product development.

Large enterprise (row 4)

Business agility: Low

Business standardization: High

Business strategy: Cost leadership

Large enterprises typically compete on cost. High business standardization allows efficient operations and cost savings. Large enterprises will typically utilize standard applications supported by standardized IT infrastructure that allows for the control and predictability of costs to the greatest extent possible. The size of the organization also influences buying decisions. Large organizations will get discounts on SAP software and its supporting hardware because they purchase in bulk. Consequently, the IT capabilities of large enterprises are highly standardized with greater focus on IT governance and service-level agreements. The enterprise architect will collaborate with IT to build standardized IT capabilities that will support the highly standardized business processes of the large enterprise.

Closing Points on IT and Business Alignment

Aligning business and IT is a continual process that matches business strategy with IT strategy. The aim is to maximize the value created by the enterprise. The following are the key takeaways from our discussion:

- Business strategy drives IT strategy planning.

- IT and business alignment is continuous; there is no final destination.

- The degree of alignment is determined by the extent to which the IT services support the business capabilities.

- IT and business alignment is measured and judged according to the business value generated from IT-enabled business processes.

- Achieving IT and business alignment ensures that the IT budget is in line with the requirements set by the business functions of the enterprise. This can be seen through

  - All IT projects speaking to proven business needs

  - All IT projects being in line with the enterprise's business strategy

  - IT investment being seen as a change enabler in the context of business strategy

Alignment Beyond Business Strategy

Thus far, the discussions have focused on aligning IT with business strategy to generate business value. It should be noted, however, that IT alignment goes beyond strategy. Cultural and budgetary realities are also areas for IT alignment. Cultural alignment refers to the organization's view of technology and aligning it in a manner that allows the organization to make the most of their IT capabilities. Budgetary alignment refers to IT costs being understood and communicated in a way that fits in with the other costs in an enterprise's budget.

Developing a Business Case

IT and business alignment are only achieved when there is complete alignment and the enterprise's IT initiatives do not deviate from business needs whatsoever. The goal is to ensure that all IT investment (every single cent) directly contributes to maximizing business value. Thorough analysis is required in determining how business processes can be IT enabled. This means developing a business case for the investment in a business process and the IT services that support it.

The business case highlights the potential value that can be realized through the investment of time, money, skills, and enterprise facilities. The business case is developed as follows.

A Business Need Is Identified

A business need for IT services/support is identified by a particular business function. The enterprise architect is tasked with evaluating this business need and assessing the potential business value it can generate through the support IT.

Analysis of Current State

The enterprise architect analyzes the current business process and the IT services that support it to confirm if they do not meet the business need. The enterprise architect must articulate how and where discrepancies exist in the current processes as any new process will have to directly speak to these discrepancies.

Collaborate on Business Case Development

In accordance with the business function's budget, the business function approves the development of a business case in collaboration with the enterprise architect. The information gathered in the analysis of the current state is used to describe the business need in terms of gaps in operational performance that result in not maximizing business value. This should be stated in monetary terms where possible. Monetary terms should also be used to express the impact of not addressing these operational gaps and how it affects the enterprise's bottom line.

Explore Alternative Solutions

Several alternative solutions should be explored. A Cost-benefit analysis must be conducted for each alternative to gain an in-depth understanding on the positives and negatives of each solution. The solutions must also be explored in other aspects beyond cost such as the degree of difficulty in managing change to facilitate their implementation or their impact on organizational culture. The cost-benefit analysis should be coupled with a calculation of the return on investment of each alternative and projection of anticipated future costs and benefits over a period of time.

Evaluation

The business case is firstly evaluated on the robustness of the analysis conducted to create it and its alignment with the goals of the business function that feed into the enterprise's strategic goals. Secondly, a financial analysis takes place to ensure the accuracy of the business case in financial terms. A recommendation is then made to the final decision makers on whether to proceed or not.

Approval/Disapproval

The relevant decision makers consider the business case in light of the enterprise's investment portfolio and business strategy. The business case must meet these five key requirements:

1.   Alignment with the enterprise's strategic goals.

2.   Clear measures and metrics for the success of the initiative.

3. The solution completely addresses the business
    need and closes the performance gaps that were
    highlighted.

4. The solution aligns with the enterprise's IT road
    map and Enterprise Architecture guidelines in
    transitioning to a future state. This is to avoid the IT
    services soon becoming redundant.

5. A cost and operational efficient implementation
    methodology has been identified.

This approval process may be combined with other regulatory
requirements that guide the business in making sound and objective
decisions regarding where it chooses to invest or not. This may be achieved
through answering questions such as

1. "How much of a priority is this potential
    investment?"

2. "Does it offer a greater return than competing
    potential investments?"

These questions move beyond examining the business case in
isolation. They consider the potential impact of implementing the changes
on the rest of the business.

If the business case is approved, funding is provided for a new
implementation project to begin. It is managed by the responsible
business function and reviewed periodically by a steering committee set
up specifically for this project. The committee takes special note of cost
and keeping schedule. A lessons-learned procedure is conducted upon
the completion of the project to help improve future project management
efforts. The solution itself is continually assessed over time to ensure that
the enterprise still derives value from it and that it still has a rightful place
in its Enterprise Architecture. The enterprise must always be vigilant about
identifying area to improve the solution or opportunities to replace it.

In the case of a disapproval, the decision may be based on a lack of economic resources, and so the project is postponed until said economic resources are available. Alternatively, the business case may not have shown the desired level of business value to justify a significant investment.

Revisiting the Four Enterprise Domains

As mentioned in Chapter 1, Enterprise Architecture has four domains:

1. **Business architecture** – Business strategy and key business processes

2. **Application architecture** – A guide for deploying individual systems

3. **Data architecture** – Documents data assets and data structures

4. **Technology architecture** – Describes the software, hardware, and IT infrastructure necessary to support applications

Throughout the sections on business strategy, IT alignment, and the enterprise architect's role in IT alignment, all of the preceding domains were explored to some degree. Business architecture was the starting point as the enterprise architect engages with business leaders on business strategy, key business processes, and governance. It is critical for the enterprise architect to develop an accurate business architecture as this is a depiction of how well they understand the enterprise and the vision of its leaders. The business architecture should be a true reflection of the enterprise's business capabilities that shows how the company generates value and how it intends on generating value in the future.

Throughout these business conversations, the enterprise architect must gain an understanding of the business processes that generate the most value. Thereafter, the enterprise architect must identify software applications that enable these essential business processes and the way they interact with each other.

The applications that support essential business processes require reliable data sources defined in the data architecture. The essential business processes and applications cannot generate business value with inaccurate, unavailable, or missing data. The enterprise architect must document the structure of logical and physical data assets and also determine rules for data governance to ensure that the data remains accurate and consistent.

Lastly, the enterprise architect works closely with IT to analyze, design, and build the IT infrastructure required to support all of the preceding architectures. The technology architecture includes networks, servers, email, Internet, and other IT services that are essential to the running of the enterprise.

Summary

In this chapter, you saw how Enterprise Architecture can be utilized in a strategic manner to create a foundation for the execution of business strategy and why an enterprise's investments in IT must be consistent with its business strategy. We delved into how Enterprise Architecture aids IT and business alignment which may lead to several benefits such as improved performance through lower costs, higher revenues, and higher returns on investment and competitive advantage through IT. IT and business alignment is a cyclical process of learning and executing; it never ends.

Enterprise architects operate at the strategic level and are the main influence on IT and business alignment. Enterprise architecture revolves around maximizing business value through ensuring that value-generating business capabilities are supported by the relevant IT capabilities. The key to success as an enterprise architect is the ability to communicate and manage different stakeholders accordingly. An enterprise architect must have an intimate understanding of the enterprise's business strategy in order to translate it into applicable IT services. EA is an alignment process, a continuous one. It is continuous because business requirements constantly change. It is a **Dynamic Alignment Process (DAP)**.

CHAPTER 3

Developing an Enterprise Architecture

Before diving into the fundamental steps of developing an Enterprise Architecture, let's briefly recap what an Enterprise Architecture is and why it is important for an enterprise to develop one. An architecture represents a collection of elements and how they relate to each other. Examples of architectures include business architectures, software architectures, hardware architectures, and network architectures. A hardware architecture will contain all of the hardware that hosts and supports the software applications utilized by the enterprise in its business operations.

Naturally, Enterprise Architecture describes the elements that make up the enterprise and how they relate to each other. The goal of Enterprise Architecture is the alignment of business and IT through establishing a common understanding of how people, business processes, and technology must collaborate to achieve a strategic business vision. Enterprise architecture is both a process and its result. It describes the vision, the steps required to achieve it, and the standards that must be maintained throughout its pursuit. An Enterprise Architecture encompasses all the above through its multiperspective view of the entire enterprise. It is a system of systems. There's precisely one Enterprise Architecture that goes to different levels of detail according to the purpose it must meet.

© Sheunopa Chalmers Musukutwa 2022
S. C. Musukutwa, *SAP Enterprise Architecture*, https://doi.org/10.1007/978-1-4842-8575-6_3

EA is a time-consuming exercise. Developing an Enterprise Architecture that delivers tangible business value requires a multidisciplinary team of architects. Despite its complexity, the Enterprise Architecture must be understandable to all stakeholders. It is for this reason that it is structured in multiple layers and perspectives with each communicating a distinct message to a specific group of stakeholders. It is the interconnectedness of these distinct messages that ultimately creates a big picture and common understanding of the business vision to all stakeholders. For instance, to business leaders, the Enterprise Architecture must be a vehicle for communicating business strategy while also being a guide for those tasked with implementation. Consequently, stakeholder engagement plays a central role in developing an Enterprise Architecture.

Developing an Enterprise Architecture is an iterative process that should result in a well-defined and repeatable program for transforming organizations in a controlled fashion. This process will include establishing an architecture framework, producing architecture artifacts, and governing the implementation of the architecture. A key part of this is establishing an enterprise-wide understanding of the word "architecture" early on.

This chapter will look at the development of the business architecture, application architecture, data architecture, and infrastructure architecture which were introduced in Chapter 1.

The Enterprise Architecture Framework

The process of developing an Enterprise Architecture is defined by an Enterprise Architecture Framework. It contains the tools, processes, principles, and templates required to create an Enterprise Architecture. The Open Group Architecture Framework (TOGAF) and the Zachman

Framework are two of the most common EA frameworks. They put forward standards, approaches, services, design, components, and concepts that guide the development of specific architectures.

The EA framework must be responsive to the enterprise's strategic goals and must therefore be founded on a thorough understanding of the enterprise's business and IT visions. It must be clear and robust enough to guide the development of the Enterprise Architecture but still be flexible enough to adapt to environmental changes over time.

Like all business and IT endeavors, it is important to understand the value to be derived from developing an Enterprise Architecture. There are "seven" reasons why developing an Enterprise Architecture is a critical step for any enterprise:

1. Gain insight into the current state of your enterprise

2. Enable the business to measure the gap between where your business is and where you would want it to be

3. Accurately align business processes with the IT processes that support them

4. Deploy enterprise-wide changes faster through established standards and governance

5. Greater accountability for and control of IT costs within the business context

6. A common language for enterprise-wide decision making, particularly on IT investments

7. Create a well-defined and clear IT landscape

So, what does it take to develop an Enterprise Architecture? The following are the two key elements required.

The Framework

- A proven methodology must be followed in architecture development.

- Recognized standards and principles must form the basis of compliance in producing architectural deliverables.

- Relevant best practice templates must guide the production of architectural artifacts.

The People

- The right skills, resources, and organizational buy-in are the most crucial aspects of developing an Enterprise Architecture.

- Stakeholder engagement and stakeholder modelling are the starting point of ensuring organizational alignment and facilitate other important steps such as requirements modelling.

- Business leaders and steering committees must deliver robust governance of the Enterprise Architecture effort.

These elements are critical when developing an Enterprise Architecture.

The Framework

This section gives a high-level overview of Enterprise Architecture Frameworks. An Enterprise Architecture Framework is a program that guides the process of Enterprise Architecture development by providing a set of practices, principles, and requirements for artifacts that describe an enterprise's architecture. It also describes how to use the resultant architecture.

As a single point of departure, the framework can be seen as a mechanism that allows a team of enterprise architects to understand each other and create the shared language required for all stakeholders to understand the enterprise vision. Creating your enterprise's EA Framework may be a matter of adapting a mainstream framework like TOGAF or the Zachman Framework, or it could mean inventing one from scratch. Adopting the EA Framework will include wording it in a way that the people in your enterprise understand and possibly going through test runs to see how well it aligns with your organizational culture.

At a minimum, components of Enterprise Architecture framework include architecture domains, standards, and a view model

Architecture Domains

The framework creates boundaries between specific architecture domains, allowing for the focus of execution while also providing the platform to depict how those specific domains interact with each other. Figure 3-1 illustrates how architecture domains are typically structured in most mainstream EA Frameworks.

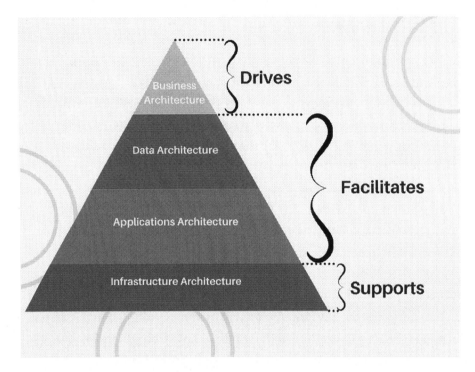

Figure 3-1. *Domain architectures*

The architecture domains in Figure 3-1 are regarded as layers that contain processes within themselves and also offer services to the layers above. This is depicted through the pyramid structure of the diagram. Each layer is supported by the one below it. The Business Architecture drives the organization's business strategy through its business capabilities. The Data Architecture and Application Architecture facilitate the execution of the business capabilities through supporting applications and data. The Infrastructure Architecture mainly includes low-level hardware such as servers, switches, and other ancillary services that support the entire enterprise. The architecture layers and how they are documented in the Enterprise Architecture will be explored in depth later in this chapter. EA implementation must be executed at a specific standard to enhance the likelihood of its success. The EA framework contains standards that guide EA implementation.

Standards

Standards form a model or measure for comparison to attain a level of quality assurance. They may be policies or guidelines the EA development process and EA itself must conform to. These policies or guidelines consist of rules that control the specification of Enterprise Architectures and the arrangement of their components. For example, an enterprise may have cybersecurity standards that include access management and password policies. In the design of the security aspect of the Enterprise Architecture, architects in conjunction with the cybersecurity team must ensure that processes are in place to ensure that these cybersecurity standards are met.

Standards may also include prescriptions of the kind of design patterns, architecture representations, architecture vocabulary, or architecture artifacts that must be utilized within a particular context. The use of an EA framework in the development of an Enterprise Architecture is a standard as there will be a notable difference between an EA developed using an EA framework and one developed with no clear frame of reference.

Different standards exist at each domain level (business, data, application, and infrastructure) and guide the decision making in the development of each architecture level to ensure it meets a specified set of requirements. Standards may include industry standards such as the ISO/IEC/IEEE 42010:2011 that sets the minimum requirements for architecture description for different contexts by providing the applicable standard terms, principles, and procedures. Once the standard is met, an Enterprise Framework may also include/augment additional tools and practices. ISO/IEC/IEEE 42010:2011 forms the foundation of most architectural frameworks as it recommends that an EA framework must be founded upon the following key elements:

- The stakeholders within the architecture

- The goals, objectives, and concerns associated with that architecture

- Architecture perspectives that cater to every stakeholder

- How those perspectives relate to each other

An enterprise architect seeks to deliver consistent IT services, adopting a standardized approach to developing products and applications. Enterprise architecture aids that effort greatly. For example, by using open-system standards, you can provide common services and create reusable building blocks. This will save the business costs and facilitate interoperability.

View Model

System specifications are generally too extensive and comprehensive to be understood by a single individual. Additionally, stakeholders have different concerns and therefore have different end goals when examining the Enterprise Architecture. Frameworks introduce different view models that facilitate stakeholder engagement by providing different viewpoints into the specification of a complex architecture. Consequently, Enterprise Architectures are inherently multidimensional and their descriptions should follow suit. An EA framework enables the creation of viewpoints that are directly relevant to stakeholders' concerns.

Enterprise Architectures must depict complex systems in a context relevant to their audiences. These audiences comprise executives, business leaders, and IT personnel. Each audience must view the Enterprise Architecture in terms that they understand and that also speak to their concerns within the enterprise. View models comprise views and viewpoints that create an approach to system analysis that is relevant to the audience analyzing the Enterprise Architecture. They allow different stakeholders to comprehend a very complex system of systems and how they relate.

Figure 3-2 depicts how different stakeholders view the Enterprise Architecture from different perspectives. Stakeholders will always view the Enterprise Architecture through their own lens which is colored by their own interests.

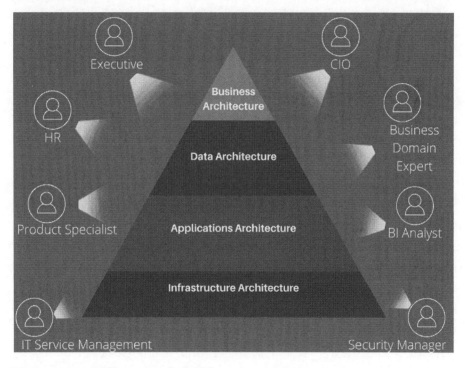

Figure 3-2. *Different stakeholder perspectives*

A view is a representation of the entire architecture through the lens of a particular group of concerns. Each viewpoint is a partitioning of the architecture according to specific stakeholder concerns. A view omits information deemed not relevant to a particular group of stakeholders while maintaining relevant information with the purpose being to simplify the Enterprise Architecture for those specific stakeholders by only addressing what concerns them. An architectural viewpoint developed to accommodate business leaders will not go in depth about supporting infrastructure such as network topologies but rather focus on business standards, processes, and principles. It may however depict how the availability of a robust network supports the business processes to achieve those business standards and abide by business principles. Viewpoints facilitate the analysis of specific areas of expertise.

Essentially, a view represents a **specification** of the architecture at a particular level of abstraction from a particular viewpoint (related set of concerns). Higher levels of abstraction are less detailed and allow the architect to understand the entire architecture. Lower levels of abstraction allow the architect to zone in on specific issues. A viewpoint model includes the objects that are part of the viewpoint but also includes the other object relationships that are relevant to that viewpoint within the system.

It is critical to understand the purpose of the architecture to direct efforts toward meeting it. Stakeholders must be able to leverage the view models in understanding the architecture within the context of their roles to deduce whether it will meet their goals. Frameworks assist as a minimum guideline for each stakeholder's interest, but the architect must still engage stakeholders to establish their specific interests in addition to the guidelines. View models provide an approach to architecture development that communicates a common and relevant understanding while remaining flexible enough to accommodate changes in the architecture.

Figure 3-3 demonstrates how customers, users, architects, and developers influence the enterprise development process differently based on their individual views.

Stakeholder	The influence of their viewpoint on EA development
Users	The concerns of users revolve around how the architecture will support them in discharging their duties. They will be influential in user acceptance testing.
Architects	Architects will be concerned about the robustness of the architecture itself and how accurately it aligns business objectives to software systems. They are interested in the correctness of the architecture as well as it's practical application.
Customers	Customer's are interested in how the architecture will enhance the service delivery of the enterprise. The revenue generated from customers influences budget, timelines and project expectations.
Developers	Developers build systems in accordance to the enterprise architecture. It forms the basis for the analysis of current systems and the decision making around the development of future systems.

Figure 3-3. *Stakeholder concerns and how they influence EA development*

Each view has only enough detail to address the concerns of the stakeholder. Customers are concerned with the high-level functions of the architecture that provide the services they expect. Users only want to see enough detail to be convinced that the resulting systems will assist them in their duties, whereas developers need enough detail to build the systems. Accommodating all these perspectives means representing the architecture in multiple views. For instance, by providing high-level focused models for the customer and user; and more detailed and elaborate descriptions for the system architects and developers.

The next section dives into one of the most popular EA frameworks, The Open Group Architecture Framework (TOGAF).

The Open Group Architecture Framework (TOGAF)

As the SAP Enterprise Architecture Framework is founded upon The Open Group Architecture Framework (TOGAF) standard, we shall have a brief look at some of its main elements. TOGAF provides adaptable EA processes, best practices, structures, guidelines, techniques, roles, artifacts, and principles that save the time of creating your own EA Framework from scratch. The guidance provided by TOGAF has been tried and tested as a framework for the designing, overseeing, and governing of Enterprise Architecture.

TOGAF provides an iterative process supported by best practices, reusable architecture assets, and tools for developing an Enterprise Architecture. TOGAF accomplishes the goal of producing robust Enterprise Architectures through establishing the following elements:

1. Introduction

2. Architecture Development Method (ADM)

3. ADM Guidelines and Techniques

4. Architecture Content Framework

5. Enterprise Continuum and Tools

6. Reference Model Library

7. Architecture Capability Framework

1. **Introduction**

   - Provides a high-level introduction to the key concepts of Enterprise Architecture including domain architectures, ADM, repositories, etc.

   - Provides definitions of common terms such as defining an "enterprise" and "Enterprise Architecture"

2. **Architecture Development Method (ADM)**

- An iterative cycle that provides repeatable processes for developing architectures.

- It consists of nine phases that guide architects in developing Enterprise Architectures:

  1. **Preliminary Phase** – Defining the principles, objectives, and requirements for a future architecture

  2. **Phase A: Architecture Vision** – Determining the scope of the architecture and the methodologies that will be utilized

  3. **Phase B: Business Architecture** – Describing an architecture vision through models

  4. **Phase C: Information Systems Architectures** – Data modelling and application architecture

  5. **Phase D: Technology Architecture** – Translating a system description into an actionable implementation plan

  6. **Phase E: Opportunities and Solutions** – Defining the main steps toward changing your current architecture to the target one, the basis of the implementation plan

  7. **Phase F: Migration Planning** – Determining timelines, required resources, road map, and costs of the implementation plan

  8. **Phase G: Implementation Governance** – Establishing governance mechanisms for architecture development

9. **Phase H: Architecture Change Management** – Providing a controlled process for implementing change

- The ADM is the most recognizable part of TOGAF including clear activities and expected inputs and outputs.

- Phases can be adapted to the extent applicable to the enterprise.

3. **ADM Guideline and Techniques**

- The guidelines provide alternatives for the application of ADM in different usage scenarios such as the use of iteration or when addressing specific requirements.

- Techniques support the tasks that are carried out in the ADM such as performing a gap analysis or risk management.

- ADM Guidelines and Techniques covers the following topics:

  1. Iteration in ADM

  2. Architecture Landscape

  3. Security Architecture

  4. SOA

  5. Architecture Principles

  6. Stakeholder Management

  7. Architecture Patterns

  8. Business Scenarios and Business Goals

9. Gap Analysis

10. Migration Planning Techniques

11. Interoperability Requirements

12. Business Transformation Readiness Assessment

13. Risk Management

14. Capability-Based Planning

4. **Architecture Content Framework**

- A model that categorizes the outputs of Enterprise Architecture development.

- It provides a checklist of architecture outputs.

- It establishes an enterprise-wide standard for the delivery of architecture outputs during ADM process.

- It provides specific examples of each content type and forms clear distinctions between artifacts, deliverables, and building blocks:

  - **Deliverables** – Normally, the work products of projects that are reviewed and signed off by stakeholders. They may form reference models for future architectural efforts.

  - **Artifacts** – Catalogs, matrices, and diagrams that are used to describe features of the architecture.

  - **Building blocks** – A package of functionality defined to meet the business needs across an organization.

5. **Enterprise Continuum and Tools**

- A model for structuring a virtual repository

- A methodology to classify solution artifacts and classify architecture

- Comprised of two inner continuums, the Architecture Continuum and Solutions Continuum

  - The Architecture Continuum categorizes outputs (deliverables, artifacts, building blocks) with regard to rules, architecture designs, representations, and relationships. The Architecture Continuum guides the Solutions Continuum.

  - The Solutions Continuum provides actual methods to implement the assets in the Architecture Continuum, leveraging technologies and frameworks. It supports the Architecture Continuum.

6. **Reference Model Library**

- Generic reference architecture models that address common business objectives.

- There are two reference models:

  - **Technical Reference Model (TRM)** – A Foundation Architecture that provides a model for generic services and functions as the foundation to more specific architecture

  - **Integrated Information Infrastructure Model (III-RM)** – A model for business application and infrastructure application

- The generic nature of TRM is a result of it categorizing services by functional area without delving into how they are implemented. This means you get a standard information system model that guides the design and development of customized information systems.

TRM and III-RM are the foundation of capturing the business environment in the framework.

They guide you in translating business criteria into a language and specifications that technology managers can understand and use. Reference models create a shared understanding that architects, managers, and all staff use to make sure development initiatives are in line with the enterprise's overall strategy. Reference models should not overly constraint Enterprise Architecture development but should be used as a guide without stifling the architect's creativity.

7. **Architecture Capability Framework**

- The Architecture Capability Framework goes over the structure, processes, skills, roles, and responsibilities required to establish and operate an architecture practice within an enterprise.

- The enterprise identifies governing bodies that will govern the Enterprise Architecture development process throughout the organization.

- An Enterprise Architecture capability is established through an architecture board, compliance reviews, contracts, governance, maturity models, and employee skills frameworks:

1. **Architecture board** – Consists of representative stakeholders that oversee the implementation of the governance strategy

2. **Compliance reviews** – A means to scrutinize the compliance of a specific project against established architectural criteria and business objectives

3. **Architecture contracts** – Agreements on the deliverables between development partners and sponsors

4. **Architecture maturity models** – Used as a comparative measure to assess the enterprise's level of architectural maturity and used as the basis for decision making in regard to the next steps in the evolution of the Enterprise Architecture

5. **Architecture skills frameworks** – Insights into the competency levels required for specific roles

When Would You Use TOGAF?

As much as TOGAF is a widely adopted framework, it is still important to ensure that it addresses the particular circumstances facing the enterprise. TOGAF can be utilized under the following conditions:

- When you need a highly detailed and standardized framework to govern your architectural transformation

- An iterative process that continually aligns your processes with current goals

- An end-to-end means for executing the architecture development process

A framework guides the enterprise in defining the architecture, but there is still a need for a clear action plan for building it in the context of your specific enterprise particularly in the context of the resources available to you such as skills, time, and cost. There are many implicit factors to take into account that may not be immediately apparent. For instance, the scheduling of the Enterprise Architecture development effort has to be structured in such a way that results can be seen early on in order to boost team morale.

The action plan should define the steps required to transition the enterprise toward its target architecture founded upon a robust modernization strategy. The next steps are to initiate the preceding Architecture Development Method by creating an architecture vision.

The Architecture Vision

The architecture vision provides an overview of how the entire enterprise will be transformed by the proposed architecture. It describes the domains of business, data, applications, and infrastructure in the context of their as-is state (baseline architecture) and to-be state (target architecture). It can be considered a preliminary document to the final architecture description but should be referenced continually during the process of Enterprise Architecture development.

This phase initiates and formalizes the Enterprise Architecture development effort as a legitimate project within the enterprise. It does this through getting the support of key decision makers through various activities such as identifying business drivers and aligning them to the architecture purpose, validating architecture principles, scoping the project, and identifying stakeholder concerns and articulating how they will be addressed. An architecture vision creates a common understanding of the project across the enterprise by communicating what needs to be done and why, not necessarily how it needs to be done at this stage. It enables stakeholders to better understand their roles within the Enterprise Architecture and how their interests will be met. The main output of this phase is a Statement of Architecture Work.

These are the questions that form a starting point for this exercise:

- What strategic goals will the architecture help in achieving?

- Who are the stakeholders and how will they use the architecture?

- What problems does the architecture aim to solve?

- Which problems are the priorities?

- What standards will we use for documenting the process?

These questions lead into an initial set of activities that will initiate the creation of an architecture vision. The objectives of this phase are to

1. Ensure that the project is adequately recognized and established within the enterprise. Line managers and other decision makers must be fully onboard.

2. Confirm the business objectives, principles, and goals driving the organization.

3. Identify relevant stakeholders and their interests.

4. Define the scope of the baseline architecture effort.

5. Identify the business requirements to be met and the constraints that must be overcome.

6. Propose an architecture definition that addresses these requirements and constraints.

7. Attain approval to proceed through articulating benefits of the EA effort to decision makers

8. Understand the impact of the project in the context of the other projects the enterprise is running

Activities must be carried out to ensure enterprise-wide acknowledgment of the project. This starts by the purpose of the architecture vision being clearly articulated. Business drivers that are linked to a return on investment motivate the stakeholders within the enterprise to pursue Enterprise Architecture development. Articulating how stakeholder interests will be met through Enterprise Architecture development is the goal of this phase. All of this will ultimately lead to gaining support from corporate and line management.

On a strategic level, there must be a thorough understanding of the business strategy and goals to bring them into synergy with the goals and objectives of the Enterprise Architecture. It is important to ensure that the business goals and drivers are documented and accepted by corporate management through validating their accuracy. If they do not exist, work with the relevant parties to define them. In similar fashion, review the architecture principles that will guide the development of the baseline architecture. Typically, these principles would have been provided by a committee tasked with creating a shared IT vision for the enterprise. The architecture vision will include a first draft of the baseline and target architectures that will be built upon going forward.

The scope of the Enterprise Architecture development effort must be defined in terms of the required level of detail, the size of the enterprise, timelines, and the architecture domains to be developed. During the scoping process, constraints must be identified, and measures of dealing with them must be put forward. It is critical to scope the Enterprise Architecture development effort accurately as this forms the basis of decision making around resource allocation and managing expectations.

Requirements engineering is a central part of developing an architecture that will ultimately align business and IT while delivering tangible value to stakeholders. Enterprise Architecture facilitates the process of requirements engineering through analyzing business processes, business cases, business drivers, capabilities, goals, and stakeholder modelling.

Identify the stakeholders and their concerns. Naturally, stakeholders will be interested in the fulfillment of business requirements that affect them directly.

TOGAF recommends the use of "business scenarios" to discover and document business requirements. The business scenario process has seven steps that can be performed iteratively to identify and analyze business needs. These business needs are used to produce business requirements that must be addressed by the Enterprise Architecture. Business requirements should be prioritized and regularly monitored. All changes to business requirements must be recorded, versioned, and audited.

Always strive to focus on the most critical and doable deliverables. The business requirements from the business scenario exercise can be prioritized according to how closely linked they are to the enterprise's strategic goals. You can also target processes that are performing inefficiently and must be optimized to address a critical business requirement. The business scenario approach also ensures that the business requirements being addressed are indeed of interest or concern to the relevant stakeholders.

Managing stakeholders is crucial to the success of Enterprise Architecture development. Architects must engage with a wide range of stakeholders (executives, implementation team, line managers) early on to gather information about how to best engage them with the appropriate level of diplomacy and cultural sensitivity. As mentioned in earlier sections of this chapter, views and viewpoints will play a critical role in providing tailored views of the architectures to keep the relevant stakeholders informed. Having open communications with stakeholders will make them feel a part of the process and facilitates any contributions they may have.

Tools such as a stakeholder matrix shown in Table 3-1 can be used to track how committed, supportive, influential, or understanding of the architecture purpose the stakeholders are.

Table 3-1. *A Stakeholder Matrix*

	Influence	Support	Understanding of EA Purpose	Contribution
Chief Executive Officer	High	Medium	High	High
Chief Financial Officer	High	Medium	Low	Medium
IT Manager	Medium	High	High	High
HR Manager	Low	Low	Low	Medium
IT Service Provider (External)	Low	High	High	Medium
Chief Auditor	Medium	Low	Low	Low

The shareholder matrix depicted in Table 3-1 identifies key stakeholders and where they stand in terms of their influence, support, understanding of the purpose of EA, and their contribution to it. This provides insight that is valuable to identifying the best way to navigate the EA endeavor.

The output of this phase is an approved Statement of Architecture Work. It details what architecture domains are to be developed and to what level of detail. A road map that includes a schedule and the required resources to complete the Enterprise Architecture development effort is included alongside a baseline architecture. A baseline architecture depicts where the enterprise is currently and provides context to the level of effort, resources, and time required to transition to a future desired state. The Statement of Architecture Work must be approved in accordance with the appropriate governance structures.

In practice, this process is not as black and white. There may be instances where this information is unavailable. This must not stop the architect from making progress. With the accumulation of information, understanding, and their own experience, the architect can make assumptions about certain aspects of the architecture at a high level. More detailed specifications can be made as the project progresses. It is very difficult for any enterprise to pull off the architecture development process in one go simply because of the rapid changes that occur in their business environments. The architecture itself must be flexible enough to accommodate change during its development to avoid being out of date by the time of its completion.

The architect must focus on the high-level aspects of the architecture vision that are closely linked to the strategic goals of the enterprise and are less likely to change due to the long-term nature of strategic goals. Lower-level aspects such as business processes that aim to deliver more immediate results must be adaptable. This is the benefit of the standardization enabled by an established framework. It is possible to change aspects of the architecture on a modular level that does not disrupt the entire architecture. Architecture is a continual process rather than an event. Implement a cycle of updating and regularly reviewing architectures; adapt them accordingly.

At the beginning of this phase, the architect must establish the following:

1. Clear lines of communication and reliable communication tools.

2. Invite participation in the process by all stakeholders.

3. Agree upon a methodology and applicable standards to govern the process.

4. Secure the support of senior management.

5. Reliable means of documenting information within and across architecture domains and business functions.

6. Avoid overscoping the project, prioritize the problems to be solved, and aim to start delivering results within six months.

7. It's a team effort. It is impossible for a single architect to articulate the architecture at all levels because it encompasses a wide array of disciplines.

An Enterprise Architecture vision ultimately determines how an enterprise views the technology that supports its business operations in meeting its business requirements and ultimately achieving the enterprise's strategic goals. Upon gaining an understanding of the framework and the architecture vision, the last and arguably the most important factor are the stakeholders.

The People

The architecture vision is essentially about deciding what to do and how much time there is to do it. The next step is selecting and organizing the people to do it on schedule. The development team should consist of up to six members headed by the chief architect. The chief architect must be a strong leader with a combination of good technical and soft skills. The development team is the focal point in connecting business and IT and so must include individuals with a strong grasp on both areas. Enterprise architects must generally have multiple skillsets as their work deals with the enterprise as a whole.

The architecture team should include system architects and functional experts in the areas within the scope of the architecture that provide specialized knowledge. The functional experts will divide their time between their daily duties and the enterprise development effort. System architects will collaborate with the functional experts and other stakeholders to develop the business requirements that they must translate into a coherent vision of what the system should do. In the case of packaged applications such as SAP, this may mean selecting the solution that most closely meets the business requirements. Furthermore, the system architects must establish how the systems will evolve and stay abreast of the latest technologies that could facilitate that evolution.

All of this will be overseen by steering committees, review boards, quality assurance teams, and conflict resolution bodies. Architecture steering committees are made up of chief architects, domain experts, and line managers. They ensure that the Enterprise Architecture development process remains on time and on budget. Steering committees assess progress and enforce corrective measures in case of any issues.

As much as there is a dedicated architecture development team, remember to invite stakeholder participation. Architecting must be an open process that stakeholders can make contributions to and ultimately facilitate buy-in. Stakeholders must be involved in the creation of deliverables, circulating drafts for review and feedback.

Figure 3-4 depicts a stakeholder hierarchy in a typical EA endeavor.

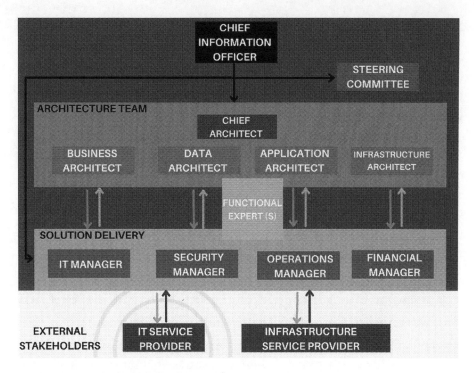

Figure 3-4. *Stakeholder hierarchy*

A stakeholder hierarchy like the one depicted in Figure 3-4 provides a quick overview of how various stakeholders relate to each other positionally and oftentimes also in terms of influence. As already highlighted, an Enterprise Architecture spans a number of disciplines that are depicted from multiple perspectives. A single architect cannot analyze, document, and articulate the Enterprise Architecture. A Business Architect is required to interpret the Strategic Plan, a Data Architect would catalog the enterprise's data, an Application Architect would design the interfaces between components, and an Infrastructure Architect is required to specify the supporting technologies. These bring about four core domain architectures:

1.   Business Architecture

2.   Data Architecture

3.   Application Architecture

4.   Technology Architecture

The Architecture

Information about an enterprise's environment is best captured by architectures or architectural views. An architecture organizes complex information in layers that are easier to understand and communicate. The common way of depicting these layers is as the business, data, applications, and infrastructure architectures. Consequently, architectures cut across domains and allow them to be seen in one view of the enterprise.

Architectures can be defined on a strategic or tactical-based level with each level becoming more focused and detailed than the last. The process of Enterprise Architecture development utilizes the concepts of a baseline architecture, a target architecture, and transitional architectures (optional).

Baseline Architecture

Developing a baseline architecture or as-is architecture is about defining the current architectural makeup of the enterprise. Some enterprises assume they do not have an architecture because they do not have a *documented* architecture. This is a common misconception. As long as there is some kind of information system in your enterprise, you have an architecture.

What information systems is the enterprise using now? This is our point of departure.

These information systems do not have to be enterprise-wide. As defined in Chapter 1, section "What Is an Enterprise?", an enterprise is people collaborating together for a purpose, supported by a platform. This means that the information system could be only serving the warehouse and procurement department but still be documented as an Enterprise Architecture.

The baseline architecture takes stock of what information systems are being used within the enterprise, their components, and the relationships between them. The baseline architecture allows you to analyze them in order to deduce their business value to the organization and the cost of running them, identify redundancies and potential for growth or replacement, and map out which users are utilizing them.

Make sure to avoid going into too much detail and describe only the critical functionality/processes of the systems that you anticipate will need replacing. Legacy systems that will not be replaced must be documented thoroughly to clearly understand how to ensure their interoperability with new systems. An architect should not spend too much time modelling baseline architectures as this is an iterative process; you will come back to them with new information based on the development process of your target architecture. Capture enough information to support your first iteration of the target architecture.

The Target Architecture

The target architecture is a description of the desired future state of the enterprise. It details the systems that the enterprise would like to implement to support business operations. Similar to the baseline architecture, the target architecture includes their interoperability, their purpose, and potential business value. The systems the enterprise would like to implement are generally improvements from the baseline architecture; there is hardly an enterprise that intends to maintain business as usual five years into the future. Consistency is important so make sure to use the same views used in the baseline architecture.

The target architecture takes future business needs into account. It should be a reflection of how the enterprise intends to evolve mainly in terms of its business architecture. The business architecture is therefore the main driver of the target architecture, whereas the baseline architecture was purely about documenting what already exists. An example of the business architecture driving the development of a target architecture is that of a traditional brick-and-mortar grocery store chain planning on introducing an end-to-end ecommerce platform in the next three to five years. This evolution in their business model will dictate the kind of technological transition they must undergo, and the target architecture will depict this.

The applications and infrastructure architectures may also drive the target architecture. For example, an enterprise may still be utilizing a legacy system or on-premise solutions but have come to realize that they may get more value out of cloud-based heterogenous solutions. Technology begins to drive the target architecture because system integration and meeting interoperability standards become critical to achieving that vision.

It is important that both the baseline architecture and target architecture development processes are iterative. This is because you are continually gathering new information and requirements are bound to change, business requirements in particular. Make sure to not get caught up in having the architecture set in stone; just make sure to gather everything relevant to the current iteration.

A target architecture is not purely an upgrade of the baseline architecture. It may be an architecture totally different to the baseline architecture; it is only seen through the same views that were used to develop the baseline architecture. The resulting document should be adequate for the planning and implementation of future systems.

The following questions can be asked to start creating a picture of what the target architecture should be:

- Are there new products the enterprise plans on introducing?

- Are there new business units dedicated to these products?

- Are the functions depicted in the target architecture sufficient to support them?

- What data/information is required to support them?

- Are existing information systems capable of supporting them?

Answers to these questions may change over time to ensure that the target architecture is adaptable. The target architecture should be in conformance to the standards and principles stated in the architectural framework. Some mistakes to avoid are insufficient analysis of business requirements and undermining the importance of stakeholder input. It should be clear that the poor analysis of existing business requirements will lead to not knowing what processes to preserve from the baseline architecture and what new processes to introduce into the architecture. Enterprises have multiple stakeholders that generally have conflicting interests. Do everything you can to gain total consensus like inviting stakeholders' input and representing the architecture in ways that all stakeholders can understand.

Transitional Architectures

Transitional architectures are an "in-between" state representing necessary transitional checkpoints in the transformational period from the baseline architecture to the target architecture. These transitional architectures must be developed with the same effort as the target architecture itself as they would have been deemed necessary for its realization. The transitions include thoroughly planned changes that involve existing and new business processes, data models, applications, and infrastructure.

We shall now look at the domain architectures. Please note that the fundamental output of all domain architectures is a baseline architecture and a target architecture.

Business Architecture

We have already spoken about the importance of business drivers under the section on architecture vision, so it should be clear that the Business Architecture is the foundation of a successful Enterprise Architecture. The business architecture encompasses why the business exists and what it does to fulfill that "why." It describes the business objectives, strategy, capabilities, and processes that must be adopted in order to achieve the target architecture. All the other architectures must understand and use the business architecture as a reference point for the end goals of architecture development. They all must enable the achievement of business value.

Furthermore, the business architecture should help executives and business leaders understand how the architecture addresses the strategic objectives. The business architecture is in essence a translation of the enterprise's mission, vision, business drivers, and strategic goals. It represents the business capabilities in the context of the enterprise's architecture. It details how the business operates in the baseline architecture and how the business needs to operate to achieve its target architecture, therefore facilitating a gap analysis.

We have already learned that IT and business alignment is fundamentally about incorporating the right technologies to best support the business capabilities and deliver business value. It is because of this that the business architecture is the focal point of IT and business alignment. The business architecture must be as accurate as possible in order to inform the decisions of the most suitable technologies required to meet business requirements. This ultimately forms the road map between the as-is and to-be states of the enterprise.

The business architecture describes who requires information and where information is required to meet business requirements. The business architecture may be further segregated into business functions such as finance, HR, or procurement to inform architects about where information systems should be located to best support them. An alternative approach would be to characterize the enterprise in terms of the products/services it delivers. This can then be elaborated upon in terms of the business processes that produce them, the stakeholders that receive and produce them, and the business units responsible for them.

As mentioned, a lot of the information of the business architecture stems from preexisting elements:

- **Strategic plan** – Strategic plans speak to the desired future of the enterprise and are essentially the basis of the direction that the enterprise seeks to go in.

- **Mission and vision** – These are almost guaranteed to exist, and they provide a succinct description of an organization's area of business and its goals.

- **Business objectives** – Business objectives or goals break down the strategy into specific terms that can be linked to the business value of the architecture. If the architecture speaks to achieving the goals, then it is easier to communicate it to the enterprise.

- **Business processes** – Business processes are a detailed description of how an organization goes about delivering its products and services. The supporting technology must be aligned with these business processes and facilitate their execution.

83

The main outputs of this process are the target business architecture, baseline business architecture, gap analysis results, technical requirements, and up-to-date business requirements. Remember that formal stakeholder reviews form an integral part of developing the business architecture as ultimately the same stakeholders will have to be convinced that the architecture speaks to their concerns. The business capabilities in the business architecture create and utilize data during transactions. The data architecture supports the business capabilities of the enterprise.

Data Architecture

The aim is to describe the important types and sources of data required to support the business, in a way that is accurate, consistent, and understandable to stakeholders. It describes the information flows and business process information to support business operations. It also describes the logical relationships and dependencies among business processes. It details how the placement and distribution of information supports users and IT applications.

It is important to note that this process is not about database design though links can be made to existing storage at the architect's discretion. Data is produced, utilized, and discarded across all domains. The flow of information fuels the business architecture, and as a result, it must be accurate, useful, and secure. Knowing which business functions leverage information, which applications serve as the master record and how the information is stored and manipulated, is integral to seeing the business processes achieve enterprise goals. A gap analysis will also take part here in regard to determining the data that the enterprise will need to carry out their target business processes.

The data architecture serves to address the following issues:

- Data in the wrong location.

- Irrelevant data.

- Data not available when required.

- Data doesn't exist.

- Data relationship gaps.

The data architecture is described by several elements.

Conceptual Data Model

This is a diagram that describes the critical data within an information system and the context in which it is deemed critical (consumers or processes that require it). The conceptual model can be produced at a business function level or across enterprises in special cases such as when an enterprise seeks to depict the flow of information in its supply chain. The diagram depicts data entities and how they relate to each other.

Logical Data Model

A logical data model depicts the makeup of data elements and how they relate to each other. The model is independent of any technology platform or specific Relational Database Management System. It does not detail how the data will be implemented, that is the physical data model. The logical data model adds more information to the conceptual model and details what data is used. It details the information that is critical to the operation of the enterprise on a day-to-day basis.

A logical data model has three main elements:

1. **Entities** – Each entity represents a set of items relevant to a business.

2. **Relationships** – Associations between entities.

3. **Attributes** – Attributes describe entities.

Given that entities describe items that are relevant to a business and relationships describe how they're associated within the context of the business, the logical data model creates a connection between business requirements and quality data structure.

Physical Data Model

Physical data models are not a must, but they may offer a useful starting point for the data architect. The data architect can use these models to deduce the logical data models and, consequently, the conceptual data models for baseline architectures. Even in scenarios when the information models were developed from the conceptual data model initially, going from the physical data model back up to the conceptual data model can be a means of double-checking the validity of the models.

The main outputs of this development process are

- Validated data principles

- Gap analysis results

- Impact analysis (areas where the Business Architecture may need to adapt to accommodate the Data Architecture)

It is important to note the importance of a robust data architecture in regard to maintaining data standards. Data is often exchanged with parties outside of the organization; standards that codify the way that data should be represented and transmitted between interested parties should be enforced.

Applications are required to enter, manage, and manipulate the data required by the business capabilities. The application architecture supports these processes.

Application Architecture

The next step is to assess the current IT applications that support the business functions. This includes documenting the data entities they utilize. The Application Architecture catalogs the applications in the enterprise describing the work that they do to capture, transform, manage, and store data. Again, this is not an exercise of application systems design but rather a high-level description (not a specification) of the applications showing logical dependencies and relationships among functional areas. The objective here is to attain an understanding of the applications critical to the enterprise's business processes and what those applications have to do to manage data and to present information to the stakeholders and computer actors in the enterprise.

The applications manage the data objects in the Data Architecture and support the business functions in the Business Architecture. The data architecture details the scope of the applications, application user groups, the applications' associations with data, and how the applications are physically distributed in different locations.

The applications are not associated with any specific technologies or service providers. What is of importance here is what the applications do to facilitate and support business operations.

The application architecture also speaks to the interfaces that are required by the applications and their interoperability. An application architect will be able to take this information and use it to develop a road map toward a target architecture. The level of detail to be defined will depend on the extent to which existing application components are likely to be carried over into the Target application architecture and on whether existing architectural descriptions exist.

The applications architecture is described by several elements.

Application Lists

This is essentially a list of applications utilized within the enterprise based on a set criteria such as being the applications in the baseline architecture. The criteria can be anything that allows stakeholders to better understand the architecture such as an application list based on functional areas that the applications are used in.

Application Diagrams

These are representations of the applications within the enterprise and how they relate to each other. A common example is an application communication diagram that depicts models and mappings related to communication between applications (e.g., application components and interfaces between components).

Application Matrices

The purpose of application matrices is to depict the relationship between applications and capabilities, the business roles and the business processes that utilize them within the enterprise. For instance, defining the applications used by a particular business role or process allows you to analyze the value of that application and whether it needs to be upgraded, replaced, or leveraged differently.

Interface Lists

Similar to the benefit of application communication diagrams, interface lists show the complexity of enterprises and how their applications are connected by depicting the number and types of interfaces between them. In the case of the baseline architecture, interface lists reveal why systems are failing when the connectedness of the applications produces a "Spaghetti diagram."

Business Processes and Applications

Applications exist for the reason of supporting business processes. Documenting the baseline architecture of how current applications support the current business processes forms the foundation of a gap analysis that will inform the effort required to achieve a target architecture. This is ideal for the identification of redundancy, duplication, and inefficiencies that may not be immediately apparent due to years of the enterprise introducing new applications and business processes to dynamically adapt to changes in its business environment.

The main outputs of this development process are

- Validated application principles

- Gap analysis results

- Applications architecture report

Infrastructure Architecture

The infrastructure (or technology) architecture is the foundation of the other architectures through providing supporting services, computing platforms, and the interfaces (interoperability) the applications need to run. The infrastructure includes descriptions of the logical, physical, and virtual infrastructure that supports the execution of application services. It is important to articulate how infrastructure meets business requirements as this is not immediately apparent to nontechnical stakeholders.

The infrastructure architecture considers the relationships between technology components (software and hardware) at a detailed level to develop what TOGAF terms as Application Platform Services. These are services that are provided to applications in a standard and repeatable way, resulting in the benefits of availability, assurance, usability, and adaptability. TOGAF's Technical Reference Model (TRM) facilitates the establishment of Application Platform Services by providing a reference of platform services.

The TRM contains architectural building blocks that create the platform for business and infrastructure applications that will provide the application and infrastructure services. Utilizing the TRM will ensure that architectures will be developed using a standard set of elements that allow for repeated and therefore standardized use. TRM allows for any type of technology, physical or virtual, to be modelled. Once the TRM is defined within the context of your enterprise, it can eventually be used as the basis for all Infrastructure Architecture models by creating instances of the infrastructure elements.

The information required for the infrastructure comes from surveying the networking infrastructure and topology, software, hardware, and telecommunications that support the systems in use. Assess the strengths and weaknesses of these components and the potential for automation. The scope of this exercise will depend on the size of the enterprise, but as a rule of thumb, identify and detail the components that support systems that execute applications for each functional area. To plan the transition of a system, you need to know the resources it requires.

Lastly, an enterprise will most likely run at multiple locations. These locations will probably be modelled within the context of the business activities that take place at those locations. In the same way, these locations also need to be articulated according to what data is located at those locations and subsequently the infrastructure required to support the collection of that data. Factors such as security , bandwidth, and performance are areas that require attention. It is important to note however that with the movement toward cloud computing, a lot of these considerations are no longer applicable with the only consideration being accessibility zones.

The main output of this development process is target infrastructure architecture.

After describing the different domain architectures, take the opportunity to get stakeholders involved by conducting a survey. First, conduct the survey before sharing the architecture in order to determine if the results are consistent with the baseline architectures. Thereafter, conduct the survey to gauge the satisfaction and understanding of the target architecture among stakeholders.

Summary

This chapter explored the process of developing an Enterprise Architecture particularly according to the Architecture Development Methodology (ADM) created by The Open Group Architecture Framework (TOGAF). The process starts off with the selection of a framework that you have determined will adequately govern and guide the development of your Enterprise Architecture development process. Frameworks come equipped with standards, principles, and best practices that you must use as a reference point to ensure the success of your project.

Subsequently, we introduced the four architecture domains of Business Architecture, Data Architecture, Application Architecture, and Infrastructure Architecture that form an efficient mechanism for organizing architectural information. The accurate and consistent development of these domain architectures is critical to the entire Enterprise Architecture effort as the gap between the baseline architectures and target architectures they produce dictates the work that must be done to transition the organization toward a future state.

Enterprise Architecture is about understanding today while planning for tomorrow while adapting your plan to new information and environmental changes you experience between those two points in time.

The next phases tackle the aspect of making the architecture work (governance) and keeping the process running. They will be explored in the next chapter within the context of SAP Enterprise Architecture as SAP has specific standards and best practices for these subsequent steps.

The following are valuable insights into the architecture development process that will help you estimate the effort accurately and avoid common mistakes:

1. Enterprise Architecture setup activities will take three to six months depending on the size of the architecture team.

2. You must have the full backing and sponsorship of the C-level executives.

3. The chief architect must be a great leader who knows how to manage expectations and stakeholder relations.

4. There must be a clear need for Enterprise Architecture and not carrying out Enterprise Architecture as a formality.

5. Members of the Architecture team must be willing to impart their knowledge and understanding on to others.

6. Give adequate consideration to external stakeholders as they are easy to forget and maybe almost as integral as some internal stakeholders.

7. The Enterprise Architecture development process is an iterative process and should be treated as such. Do not dwell on activities for too long as you will likely be conducting them again.

CHAPTER 4

Enterprise Architecture and SAP

Thus far, we have established that there are various frameworks, including the SAP Enterprise Architecture Framework, that can be used to govern Enterprise Architecture. These frameworks have risen to prominence because

- They have been utilized across industries.

- They are vendor-agnostic.

- They are applicable to many types of architectures.

- They give Enterprise Architects a solid point of departure and act as a guideline.

- They can be customized to meet the needs of different types of enterprises.

- They have comprehensive architecture development methods.

Above all else, these frameworks have survived the test of time because they have been proven to work. It is for this reason that the logical question to ask is what justification is there for SAP to insist on its own iteration of an Enterprise Architecture Framework. This chapter discusses the SAP Enterprise Architecture Framework (SAP EAF), beginning with a review of the history of Enterprise Architecture specifically in regard to

© Sheunopa Chalmers Musukutwa 2022
S. C. Musukutwa, *SAP Enterprise Architecture*, https://doi.org/10.1007/978-1-4842-8575-6_4

SAP and how it has developed to empower SAP customers in executing successful implementations. We'll then examine the components of the SAP Enterprise Architecture Framework at a glance before getting a taste of the SAP Enterprise Architecture Designer. The chapter concludes by returning to the Architecture Development Method and exploring its remaining stages.

SAP and EA: A Brief History

Historically, Enterprise Architecture has been a highly technical endeavor best suited for custom development and not necessarily suited for packaged business applications. As Enterprise Architecture matured to become more business driven, it expanded from just documenting IT systems to becoming more forward thinking in regard to optimizing IT investments. The maturity of EA allowed for a shift in the software market toward packaged business solutions because of four key investment-related reasons:

- Packaged solutions mean lower risk and uncertainty. Customers are aware of cost implications, timelines, and deliverables ahead of time. This allows for increased governance, transparency, and predictability.

- The functionality and value of packaged solutions are easier to understand and articulate to stakeholders even ahead of time; this increases the chances of success.

- Packaged solutions are modularized to allow organizations to only purchase the functionality they need which leads to lower cost and faster time to value.

- (In fact, with the growth of integration capabilities, some enterprises will have several vendors providing software modules to specific departments, creating a heterogenous environment. Enterprise Architecture becomes of even more value in such environments.)

- In recent times, cloud computing has strengthened the demand for packaged solutions through the availability of subscription-based services, a lower barrier to entry which increased the number of service providers, and all of these have resulted in lower risk and lower costs.

Expensive open-ended enterprise software development carries a lot of risk. The failure of IT projects has been widely publicized with most projects experiencing cost overruns, running behind schedule, and ultimately turning out to be misaligned with business goals. Packaged solutions came to being as a response to the market demand for lower costs, shorter implementation cycles, and less uncertainty. Software vendors such as SAP developed module-based packaged solutions that could be implemented in phases which allowed for greater management and control which lead to more predictable results.

Packaged business solutions were now a part of the multiple deployment routes an organization can take in order to implement systems that align with their business objectives. Naturally, SAP felt that there was a need for an architecture with a specific focus on their packaged solutions. In order to support the achievement of all the benefits of their packaged business solutions, SAP both adapted existing and created its own standards, methodologies, and governance structures adapted to SAP's packaged business solutions. Today, there has been a continuous refinement of this approach, resulting in what SAP calls its rapid deployment solutions – preconfigured applications with a standardized implementation approach and the required materials to support it that results in a drastically shorter implementation time.

Generally speaking, preexisting EA frameworks can support SAP customers' digital transformation and business-IT alignment initiatives, but the SAP Enterprise Architecture Framework maps directly to SAP's methods, services, and tools (such as SAP Enterprise Architecture Designer which we shall introduce in this chapter.)

Beyond packaged business solutions, SAP EAF was also introduced to support the integration of Service-Oriented Architecture (SOA) patterns. SOA has many definitions but is generally an approach to software design in terms of services. A service can be considered as an activity with a specific outcome. It is a unit of functionality that can be accessed and executed over a network. It performs automated tasks, responds to hardware events, or listens for data requests from other software, for example, an API. A service can exist independently or be part of a larger group of services that collectively provide a specific outcome or provide the functionality of a software application. SAP EAF explicitly addresses the content that package-enabled SOA solutions offer in general – and the SAP-specific content in particular.

Over the years, SAP customers have utilized Enterprise Architecture as a tool for aligning business and technology initiatives throughout their organizations. SAP applications are typically only one part of the technology landscapes overseen by IT executives, managers, and solutions architects. The goal is to equip readers with the knowledge to thrive in such environments by providing a foundational understanding of Enterprise Architecture.

SAP customers can make informed and relevant decisions on strategic business transformation projects that speak to the "to-be" state articulated by EA. Standards, guidelines, and service-level agreements must be documented for the deployment and maintenance of these applications. This process is simplified in the case of packaged solutions as solution providers such as SAP have existing best practices and service-level agreements.

Overall, SAP EAF takes TOGAF and focuses it on SAP solutions to empower enterprises in implementing SAP solutions at a lower cost, with minimal risk and higher chances of success.

The SAP Enterprise Architecture Framework

The SAP Enterprise Architecture Framework was officially launched in 2007 and is based on The Open Group Architecture Framework (TOGAF). It essentially comprises supplementary information, optimized content, and artifacts intended to accommodate packaged business solutions and Service-Oriented Architecture (SOA). SAP leaned on its decades of experience with prepackaged business solutions to formally document how to navigate the critical stages within the architecture process.

Similar to TOGAF, SAP EAF delivers a framework for an iterative process for the entire enterprise that is specifically mapped to SAP methodology. The SAP EAF accelerates architecture creation by providing best practices and artifacts that are relevant to its solutions and would normally have to be developed from scratch. Additionally, it provides the structure to store and arrange the architecture in a way best suited for SAP solutions and also one that is conducive for articulating the architecture to stakeholders.

SAP EAF empowers enterprises to drive business change through tailored implementations that focus on smaller rapid projects. It is important to note that this was also SAP's response to the growing popularity of agile methodologies. Historically, implementations were generally long-term (and costly) endeavors best suited to the Waterfall methodology. SAP's previous implementation methodology, ASAP methodology, was a traditional Waterfall method. With the growth of agile methodologies, SAP now has the improved Activate methodology to accommodate more flexible and rapid development.

Ultimately, the SAP EAF saves the enterprise time and effort leading to lower costs. Namely, the SAP EAF includes the following elements:

- **Accelerators** – Blueprints and examples that give a quick start for specific EA scenarios

- **Road maps** – Helps optimize business value and the return on your IT investment by describing how the capabilities of an SAP solution are planned to progress over time

- **Reference architecture documentation** – A blueprint of recommended structures and integrations of IT products and services to form a solution

- **Templates** – Models and prototypes that help structure the individual steps of the EA process

- **EA modelling tools** – Tools such as SAP Enterprise Architecture Designer used to capture architecture layers and requirements

The SAP EAF itself can be further adapted to suit different engagement models. SAP EAF provides predefined architecture patterns for different architecture development styles. Iterations can be defined and executed in a way that best suits the enterprise's circumstances.

Figure 4-1 offers an overview of the SAP Enterprise Architecture Framework.

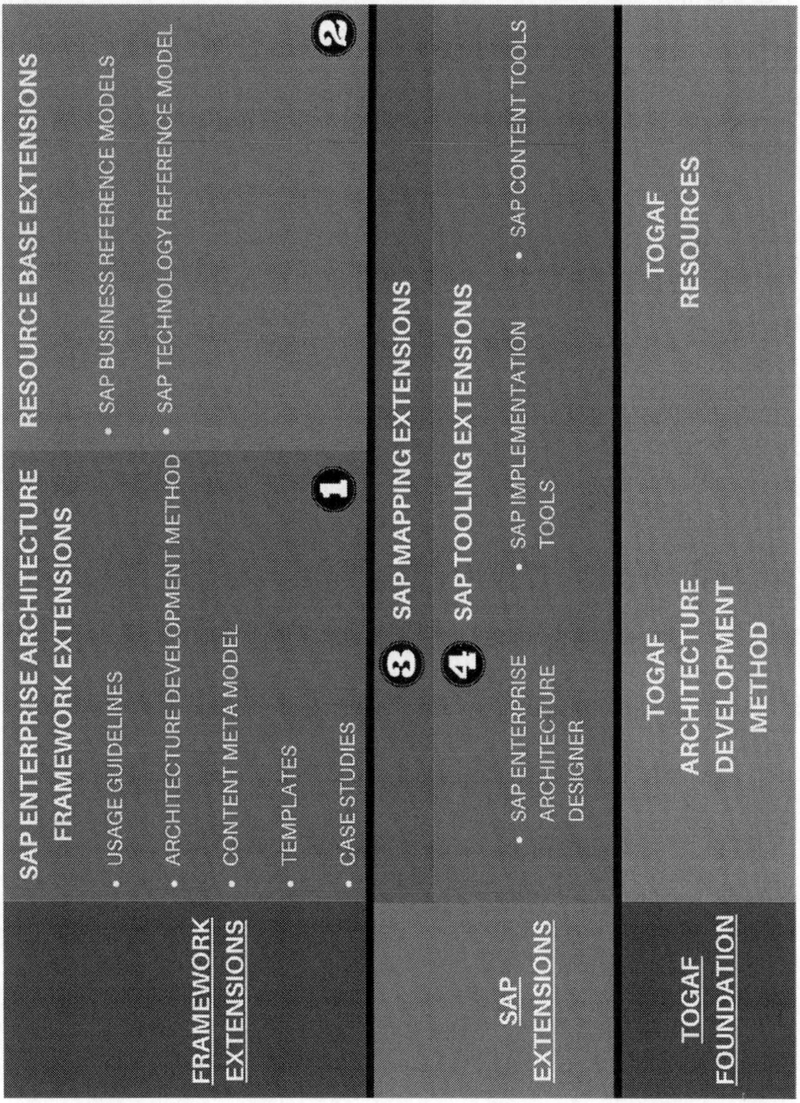

SAP ENTERPRISE ARCHITECTURE
FRAMEWORK EXTENSIONS

RESOURCE BASE EXTENSIONS

- USAGE GUIDELINES
- ARCHITECTURE DEVELOPMENT METHOD
- CONTENT META MODEL
- TEMPLATES
- CASE STUDIES

- SAP BUSINESS REFERENCE MODELS
- SAP TECHNOLOGY REFERENCE MODEL

FRAMEWORK EXTENSIONS

SAP MAPPING EXTENSIONS

SAP TOOLING EXTENSIONS

- SAP ENTERPRISE ARCHITECTURE DESIGNER
- SAP IMPLEMENTATION TOOLS
- SAP CONTENT TOOLS

SAP EXTENSIONS

TOGAF ARCHITECTURE DEVELOPMENT METHOD

TOGAF RESOURCES

TOGAF FOUNDATION

Figure 4-1. *SAP Enterprise Architecture Framework overview*

Figure 4-1 depicts the TOGAF foundation that the SAP EAF is based on. It then shows the framework and SAP Extensions that added to the TOGAF foundation to adapt it to suit SAP solutions:

1. **SAP Enterprise Architecture Framework Extensions**

   User guidelines

   – Framework adaptation

   – Engagement initiation

   – Business capability assessment

   – Technology capability assessment

   – IT governance impact assessment

   – Solution architecture scoping

   Architecture method

   – Iterative architecture process extending TOGAF ADM

   – Worksheet for each architecture phase identifying inputs, steps, and outputs

   – Steps for each architecture phase explaining how to conduct the phase

   Case studies and examples

   – Case studies from real-world SAP architecture engagements

   – Examples for all defined architecture views and matrices

   – Candidate architecture principles

Content metamodel

- Architecture metamodel, aligned with TOGAF terms

- Defined set of architecture catalogs, views, and matrices

2. **Resource base extensions**

- SAP business maps

- SAP-TOGAF TRM reference model

- SAP product availability matrix

- SAP reference model content

- Reusable models and patterns

- Use directly or as template

3. **SAP Mapping Extensions**

- SAP Enterprise Architecture Framework terminology to SAP terminology mapping

- SAP product to TOGAF TRM mapping

- SAP Enterprise Architecture Framework method to SAP method mapping

4. **SAP Tooling Extensions**

- Enables EA tool mapping

Benefits of an SAP-specific Architecture Framework

- Enables SAP-specific mapping through formalizing the relationships between objects

- Allows the use of SAP reference models

- Enables EA tool mapping

- Allows a "quick start" for an EA tool implementation alignment between SAP end-to-end business processes and technology

- Formalizes the definition of your Enterprise Architecture

- Aids communication and understanding leading to more effective knowledge sharing across the whole organization

- Clearer business-IT traceability and alignment

- Uses SAP's product architecture standards promoting standardization and reuse

- Easier maintenance of architecture as the business and IT landscape changes

- Provides stakeholders with models most relevant to their role

The next section will dive into how SAP customers can leverage SAP EAF.

How Can SAP EAF Be Used by SAP Customers?

SAP solution implementations require major investments in terms of time, money, and skills. This is further complicated by the existence of multiple deployment options. SAP customers require a clear vision of what a successful implementation should look like as well as the guidelines, standards, and governance that leads to a successful implementation. The SAP Enterprise Architecture Framework provides the big picture and framework to select the best deployment option through an understanding of the potential impact of change, the risks each deployment option faces, and ultimately making decisions based on quantitative evidence.

The benefits of utilizing the SAP Enterprise Architecture Framework are aligned with the benefits of using an Enterprise Architecture framework in general with the key differentiator being that the SAP EAF has SAP-specific content which ultimately enables customers to create a more accurate architecture vision. On the same note, SAP customers utilize the SAP EAF for similar reasons to any other Enterprise Architecture endeavor:

- **Facilitating digital transformation** – SAP EAF facilitates business strategy–based, enterprise-wide digital transformation and business strategy–driven business and IT alignment.

Facilitating Digital Transformation

The "why" of digital transformation is arguably more important than the "how." As discussed throughout this book, the starting point of any Enterprise Architecture is the business strategy. The business strategy describes where the business wants to go, and, subsequently, the business can determine how a digital transformation will support that. SAP customers invest heavily to enable crucial business transformations driven by SAP solutions.

SAP customers generally pursue a business transformation to

- Transform service delivery to their customers (e.g., SAP CRM, SAP Hybris)

- Transform internal operations (e.g., SAP S/4HANA)

- Develop their IT capability to a high standard

SAP implementation methodologies generally include a business blueprint stage whose end product is a document that details how the enterprise does business, future business processes, and business requirements. In a typical implementation, everything is done within the context of the SAP solution and to address an immediate need. However, an enterprise-wide digital transformation considers the entire enterprise and how the new business processes, applications, information, and infrastructure are integrated. So, similar to the business blueprint stage in an SAP implementation, an enterprise-wide digital transformation also requires a blueprint that not only considers SAP solutions but every other component of the enterprise.

If SAP solutions make up the core of the IT landscape, it makes sense to utilize a framework that has SAP at its core but remains sufficient to cater to other IT solutions and other components of your enterprise. Elements such as SAP business maps or reference model content may be specific to SAP, but the execution methods such as the architecture development method or business capability assessment can be utilized in any environment.

As it will be shown later in the book, tools such as SAP Enterprise Architecture Designer can build an enterprise-wide model of the as-is IT architecture in terms of business, data, application, and infrastructure framework layers.

SAP EAF enables organizations to

- Capture business processes in a standardized fashion that can later be used as a basis of integration

- Build models that depict an as-is Enterprise Architecture model plus simulation and analysis of the competing to-be scenarios to support the business cases for digital transformation

- Develop EA metric-based trade-off diagrams that provide a graphical representation of the different deployment options

Ultimately, SAP EAF empowers the SAP customers in making informed decisions about their digital transformations.

Business Strategy–Driven Business and IT Alignment

SAP solutions are prepackaged business solutions that must simply be installed and configured. The advantage of this is the accelerated implementation time in comparison to custom development. However, it becomes critical that SAP customers select SAP solutions with the right functionality to support their business requirements without any need for costly additional custom development. SAP customers must utilize SAP EAF to ensure the alignment of business and IT within the context of their SAP solutions and within the context of their enterprise-wide long-term vision.

The first step in achieving this alignment is encouraging the ownership of SAP solutions by business. SAP solutions are typically seen as the responsibility of IT with IT being solely responsible for SAP solutions meeting business requirements. In practice, SAP solutions play a critical part in the ability of business to meet its day-to-day objectives, so input and feedback from business will be the difference between alignment and misalignment. Encouraging ownership starts by articulating the architecture in a way that business understands. SAP EAF maps SAP terminology to the business terminology business people understand. Real-world case studies give business people reference points that speak to their realities. Once business understands the architecture in their terms, they can see the importance of the alignment effort.

Secondly, having a way to translate SAP terminology into business terminology and vice versa facilitates communication between business and IT. Business and IT can collaborate in a way they both understand and, more importantly, in a way that focuses on the big picture especially given that the foundation of SAP EAF is the business strategy and goals. This is the multiperspective aspect of Enterprise Architecture; it allows stakeholders to interact with it in a manner that best speaks to their roles in the enterprise.

Thirdly, the standardized content and iterative architecture process provided by SAP EAF enable organizations to recognize overlapping projects, a duplication of effort or areas for synergy. When the whole enterprise speaks the same language within the context of the enterprise's architecture, ensuring that all business capabilities are sufficiently supported and that all IT capabilities are indeed supporting the business capabilities becomes much simpler. SAP EAF includes EA tools that help with the modelling and documenting of an Enterprise Architecture. The next section introduces such a tool, SAP Enterprise Architecture Designer, and its role in the EA process.

SAP Enterprise Architecture Designer

In the context of SAP Enterprise Architecture Framework, architecture is the modelling of the enterprise that is used for activities such as change impact analysis, requirements analysis, and cost/effort estimation in order to plan and execute successful implementation projects. It allows the enterprise to have a clear understanding of the benefits and the issues of a specific endeavor before any implementation work is ever done. The information is articulated from multiple perspectives to accommodate all stakeholders becoming a single source of truth. Modelling visualizations depict the interdependencies that exist throughout the enterprise which may have not been immediately apparent to individual stakeholders.

The SAP Enterprise Architecture Designer (SAP EAD) is the tool responsible for developing the architecture. The SAP EAD is a user-friendly central platform that maintains and integrates the organization's business, data, application, and infrastructure layers within a heterogenous environment. SAP EAD is a web-based collaborative tool that stakeholders in different roles can access and use. This book has emphasized the importance of stakeholder involvement; such a tool gives all relevant stakeholders the opportunity to participate directly in the planning and design of the architecture.

Governance rules and standards can be implemented on this central platform to ensure that all architecture activities and architecture changes adhere to them. This supports compliance from the very beginning of the Enterprise Architecture endeavor. SAP EAD enhances the understanding of the objects in the environment and the relationships between them. This is important for activities such as change analysis. Any change to an infrastructure object should be fully understood not only in its own context but also in the context of the related business, application, or data objects. Reports of this sort of analysis can be generated and distributed to interested parties. EA Designer is available both on-premise and in cloud versions for deployment.

The following artifacts can be created in SAP EAD:

- **Requirements list** – A list of business objectives, business needs, and functional requirements. This allows you to create or import a list of business or technical requirements and link them to other artifacts in your landscape.

- **Business Architecture** – Includes BPMN diagrams, business process diagrams for the analysis of business processes.

- **Data models (conceptual data model editor and physical data model editor)** – Depict the conceptual structure of information systems supporting insights into the objects they comprise. Document the business and physical data definitions for compliance communication throughout the enterprise. Document both SAP and non-SAP data landscape. SAP HANA database structures can be generated based on these models.

- **Data flow diagrams (data movement model editor)** – These diagrams depict the flow of data through a system and its processes.

- **Enterprise Architecture** – Lastly, the enterprise Architecture itself. It documents the enterprise, organizational charts, business processes, business capabilities, systems, IT capabilities, and infrastructure. This forms the basis for business transformation planning.

The three cornerstones of the SAP Enterprise Architecture Designer are its ability to

- Translate business strategy into technical implementation requirements

- Generate architecture and technical artifacts automatically

- Enable collaboration across the enterprise

All relevant users can access the central tool to execute the activities they're responsible for and which can be subsequently utilized as input for the next step in the architecture development process. SAP EAD as an end-to-end tool is illustrated in Figure 4-2.

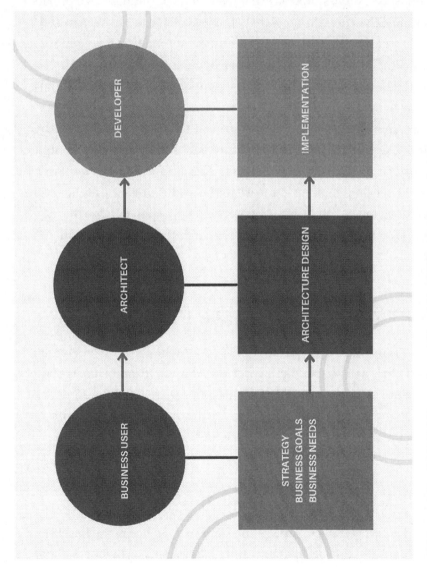

Figure 4-2. *SAP EAD can be utilized by different types of users*

Figure 4-2 depicts how different types of users can utilize SAP EAD for their specific end goals. The business user can document business strategy within the business architecture domain, whereas the enterprise architect can use SAP EAD to develop models. The outputs of the preceding processes are architectures, plans, and designs that can be utilized by different stakeholders such as executives, auditors, and service providers.

SAP EAD has functionality that enables collaboration such as the ability to share models via email, comment on models, create reports, and generate implementation code to share with development teams.

As the Enterprise Architecture is essentially a living asset that must continue to evolve alongside the enterprise and its environment, SAP EAD remains useful by facilitating the evolution of the architecture by continuously managing the architecture. SAP EAD graphically compares versions of models and architectures to support the analysis required for informed decision making in regard to the evolution of the architecture.

In the following chapters (Chapters 5–7), we shall explore the functional capabilities of SAP Enterprise Architecture Designer in more detail.

Returning to the Iterative Process

SAP EAF is inspired by TOGAF. The TOGAF Architecture Development Method phases described in the previous chapter form the basis of the iterative processes in SAP EAF. The next phases are the differentiator because they tackle the aspect of making the architecture work and keeping the process running within an SAP context specifically.

Opportunities and Solutions

Once an enterprise goes through the steps of developing the baseline architecture and the target architecture in terms of the business, data, application, and infrastructure layers, the enterprise must now evaluate the best deployment option to take. The enterprise can now decide on the specific projects to be undertaken in transitioning toward the target architecture. Important factors such as budget, timelines, and dependencies come into play, and the model comparison functionality of the SAP EAD take center stage.

In TOGAF's ADM, this phase may include making a decision or decisions about custom development, packaged solutions, or reuse. In the context of SAP, there are prepackaged business solutions that will address business needs and the sub-options available such as on-premise or cloud implementations. Furthermore, this stage seeks to identify new business opportunities based on insights from the architecture work that has been carried out. Ultimately, the outcome of this stage will be the foundation of the implementation plan required to move to the target architecture.

The gap analysis between current business processes and the target business processes conducted in the earlier stages directs this phase by highlighting the missing functionality that will have to be purchased and implemented. Logical groupings of the required functionality allow us to separate them into specific projects aligned with the business strategy. For instance, functionality that is related to the sharing of data across the organization may lead to an integrated ERP system like SAP S/4HANA. All of this information will also help to determine whether an incremental approach is required and therefore initiate the development of transition architectures that will ensure the continuous delivery of business value.

Based on the gap analysis, there is likely to be a great emphasis on the implementation of missing functionality. It is important to not forget the current functionality that already exists but may need to be updated or replaced in order to better serve the enterprise. There are recommended steps in identifying the opportunities and solutions available to an enterprise during the EA process.

The opportunities and solutions include the following steps:

1. Determine/confirm key corporate change attributes.

2. Determine business constraints for implementation.

3. Review and consolidate gap analysis results from earlier stages.

4. Review consolidated requirements across related business functions.

5. Consolidate and reconcile interoperability requirements.

6. Refine and validate dependencies.

7. Confirm readiness and risk for business transformation.

8. Formulate implementation and migration strategy.

9. Identify and group major work packages.

10. Identify transition architectures.

11. Create the architecture road map and implementation and migration plan.

The outputs of this phase include the following:

- Draft architecture requirements specification

- Capability assessments

- Architecture road map including identification of transition architecture

- First parts of implementation and migration plans

Migration Planning

This stage is a consolidation of the previous stage that results in a final architecture road map including the implementation and migration plans that support it. The enterprise must ensure that the architecture road map is aligned with how it manages change within the organization. SAP EAF offers templates for developing these plans in different scenarios and in the context of different organizational cultures. Having a central tool such as SAP EAD enables the necessary collaboration between project managers, project sponsors, and portfolio managers required to develop the implementation plan.

The implementation and migration plans provide a schedule for implementation of the solution described by the architecture road map. The implementation and migration plans include timing, cost, resources, benefits, and milestones for the implementation.

It is important to note that the architecture road map has been developed since earlier stages of the iterative process; it is now being finalized at this stage with all factors from each stage being taken into consideration.

Migration planning includes the following steps:

1. Confirm management framework interactions for the implementation and migration plans.

2. Assign a business value to each work package.

3. Estimate resource requirements, project timings, and availability/delivery vehicle.

4. Prioritize the migration projects through the conduct of a cost/benefit assessment and risk validation.

5. Confirm architecture road map and update architecture definition document.

6. Complete the implementation and migration plan.

7. Complete the architecture development cycle and document lessons learned.

The outputs of this phase include the following:

– Implementation and migration plans including implementation strategy, migration strategy, and project charters

– Finalized architecture definition document

– Finalized architecture requirements specification

– Finalized architecture definition document

Implementation Governance

Implementation Governance is about building a repository of all of the information or successful management of the various implementation projects. The implementation must follow the enterprise's standards for corporate, IT, and architecture governance. SAP EAF provides standards, principles, and guidelines specific to SAP solutions which enable the enterprise to take a more focused approach. Implementation Governance goes beyond the implementation as one of its goals is also to define an operations framework for the maintenance of the solution.

The enterprise must endeavor to perform the governance functions stipulated in the architecture contract to govern the overall implementation and deployment process. SAP Enterprise Architecture Designer's central administration functionalities utilize permissions to ensure the security and integrity of all architectural assets. SAP EAD can be configured to ensure that changes to any architectures go through a specific approval workflow before they can be published. It also assigns version numbers to each updated architecture which may be used to return to an older version or for comparison capabilities such as

- To compare two versions of the same model

- To compare existing published models

- To compare current draft models

Architecture owners are notified by email about any comments made on their models. The governance functionality of SAP EAD can be summarized as follows:

- Perform impact analysis within and across models

- Share common artifacts to reduce redundancy

- Approve models through a controlled workflow

- Manage user rights, permissions, and track activities

Implementation Governance is also crucial to the next stage (Architecture Change Management) because it is critical that the governance body establishes criteria to determine whether a change request warrants just an architecture update or whether it warrants starting a new cycle of the Architecture Development Method.

Implementation Governance includes the following steps:

1. Confirm scope and priorities for deployment with development management.

2. Identify deployment resources and skills.

3. Guide development of solution deployment.

4. Perform Enterprise Architecture compliance reviews.

5. Implement business and IT operations.

6. Perform post-implementation review and close the implementation.

The outputs of this phase include the following:

–   Signed architecture contract

–   Compliance assessments

–   Change requests

–   Architecture-compliant solutions

Architecture Change Management

Architecture Change Management is about ensuring that all changes are carried out in conformance to the governance standards. This includes assessing any formal change requests to decide on whether the enterprise should initiate a new architecture evolution cycle. This process will typically provide for the continual monitoring of such things as governance requests, new developments in technology, and changes in the business environment. One of the advantages of Enterprise Architecture is that it enables an organization to rapidly adapt to change. Architecture Change Management facilitates this by having clearly defined steps that ensure that a need for potential change can be detected, assessed, and deployed.

Architecture Change Management forms the basis of the Enterprise Architecture being a living document by facilitating its evolution. It is Architecture Change Management that is responsible for the enterprise responding to new business needs and therefore adjusting the Enterprise Architecture accordingly. Once again, SAP EAD's impact analysis capabilities, SAP's business, and reference technical models provide value since they provide insight into the impact of potential changes or provide reference models for executing the change in the context of SAP solutions.

It is important to note that the architecture itself may continue to suit an organization while the underlying solutions no longer do so. An architect must be able to pick this up by identifying where solutions are no longer delivering business value and a change is required. Understandably, Architecture Change Management must be integrated with performance management and reporting to record both pre- and postchange analyses. If a particular change will have a high impact on the enterprise, then a separate strategy to manage its high impact must be defined.

In the final analysis, the Architecture Change Management is about determining the scenarios under which the Enterprise Architecture will be allowed to change after it has been implemented and the process by which that will happen.

Architecture Change Management includes the following steps:

1. Establish a value realization process.

2. Deploy monitoring tools.

3. Manage risks.

4. Provide analysis for Architecture Change Management.

5. Develop change requirements to meet performance targets.

6. Manage the governance process.

7. Activate the process to implement change.

The outputs of this phase include the following:

–   Architecture updates (for maintenance changes)

–   Changes to the architecture framework and principles (for maintenance changes)

–   New request for architecture work, to move to another cycle (for major changes)

117

Summary

As much as there are more popular and established Enterprise Architecture frameworks, none of them were developed specifically within the context of packaged solutions. The TOGAF-inspired SAP Enterprise Architecture Framework provides a wealth of information and tools specific to packaged business solutions that accelerate architecture development and implementation. The SAP EAF can mainly be used to facilitate

1. Business strategy–based, enterprise-wide digital transformation

2. Business strategy–driven business and IT alignment

The first half of the architecture development method is primarily concerned with developing the architecture, whereas the second half is focused on deploying and maintaining it. It is at this stage that it becomes critical to narrow it down to SAP-specific best practices, standards, tools, and reference models in order to increase the enterprise's chances of success. Tools such as the SAP Enterprise Designer greatly enhance an enterprise's ability to create, maintain, collaborate, and govern an enterprise's architecture.

The next chapter will explore how SAP Enterprise Designer facilitates the architecture modelling process of the Business Architecture domain.

CHAPTER 5

Developing Business Architecture Using SAP Enterprise Architecture Designer

In the opening chapter of this book, we highlighted that one of the aspects that makes Enterprise Architecture unique is that it is both the process and the output, the journey and the destination. Business Architecture includes both the description of the structure of an organization and the design process undertaken to describe the organization. It forms the foundation of every other domain architecture, namely, the data, application, and technology architecture. Similar to all other forms of architecture, the foundation is the most critical area to get right.

A well-articulated Business Architecture forms the basis for a common language that is crucial to drive business discussions and ultimately communicate the strategy of the business in a way that all stakeholders can understand. It can also be crucial in terms of managing organizational change as it can communicate the value and expected impact of Enterprise Architecture.

© Sheunopa Chalmers Musukutwa 2022
S. C. Musukutwa, *SAP Enterprise Architecture*, https://doi.org/10.1007/978-1-4842-8575-6_5

Fundamentally, Business Architecture provides a description of a business organization, and SAP Enterprise Architecture Designer can be leveraged as a tool for constructing this description. This chapter explores business architecture within the context of SAP EAD.

The business architecture must support the business strategy and business model. Figure 5-1 illustrates this concept.

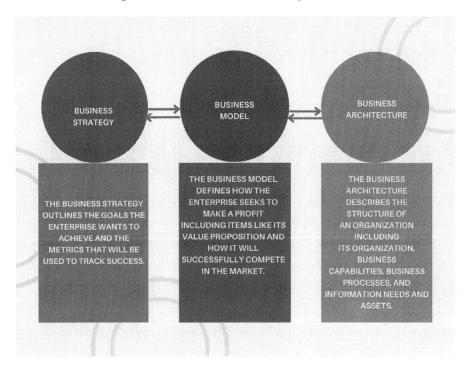

Figure 5-1. *The roles of business strategy, the business model, and business architecture*

Figure 5-1 highlights the roles of Business Strategy, Business Model, and Business Architecture to distinguish them from one another while also showing how they are related. For instance, the Business Strategy details the goals of the organization, the Business Model outlines how those goals will be achieved, and the Business Architecture describes the structure,

capabilities, and information assets required to execute the business
model and achieve the business's strategic goals.

- The Business Strategy outlines the goals the enterprise
  wants to achieve and the metrics that will be used to
  track success.

- The Business Model defines how the enterprise seeks
  to make a profit including items like its value proposition and how it will successfully compete in the market.

- The Business Architecture describes the structure of an
  organization including its organization, business
  capabilities, business processes, and information
  needs. It generally comprises

  - Business capabilities

  - Business processes

  - Information needs

  - Business structure

SAP EA Designer captures all of these elements in a manner that allows
for analysis, visualization, and the management of change. The following
sections will look at the functionality and objects SAP EAD utilizes to
model these elements.

Business Capability Modelling

Business capabilities are an enterprise's ability to carry out business
functions and achieve business objectives while delivering value to
its customers. Business capabilities are seen purely from a business
perspective and dictate what an enterprise has to do in order to succeed.
A business capability model is used to graphically represent business
capabilities in terms of their hierarchy and relationships.

SAP EAD can visualize capabilities per business function as shown in the following for the sales capability. Figure 5-2 depicts an example in which the Sales capability contains subcapabilities:

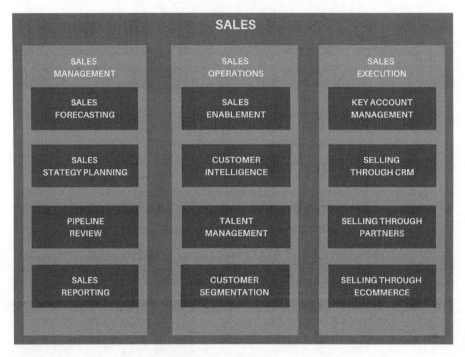

***Figure 5-2.** Business capability models*

The different business capabilities can then be brought together for all functions and prioritized through color-based heat mapping as shown in Figure 5-3.

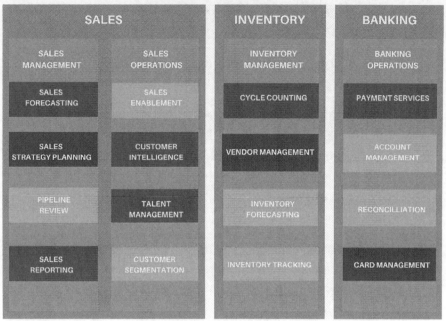

Figure 5-3. *Color-based heat mapping in business capability models*

SAP EAD provides all the functionality required to create a business
capability model as shown in Figure 5-2. The business capability model
can be exported to Microsoft PowerPoint.

This ultimately allows for business-focused discussions and
evaluations that form the basis of decision making as it becomes clear
what business capabilities the enterprise should focus on. All key
decision makers can analyze the enterprise's capabilities from a common
perspective and therefore communicate in a common language. Business
capability mapping aligns strategy and execution because it articulates
what has to be done in the business. Please take note that it defines what
has to be done, not how.

Once we have modelled the business capabilities, we can now proceed
to enable those business capabilities with three supporting elements:

1. The right human resources and organizational
   structure.

2. The relevant business processes required to carry
   out the business capabilities. Process groups are
   a collection of business processes that allow for
   logical grouping. Business processes are linked
   to Business Process Model and Notation (BPMN)
   diagrams for further analysis.

3. The technological assets and infrastructure
   required. Business capabilities can be associated
   with applications that support their realization.

Figure 5-4 is a graphical depiction of the supporting role of the three
supporting elements and how they enable business capabilities that are
part of your business architecture.

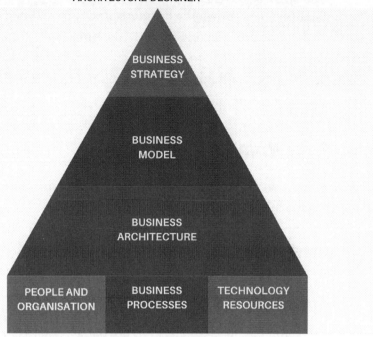

Figure 5-4. *Enabling business capabilities*

Business Process Modelling

Business processes can be defined as a collection of structured and related activities that are performed to accomplish a business goal. Inputs are transformed into outputs to create value. Business capabilities say what an enterprise has to do, business processes detail how it goes about doing them. Business capabilities are relatively stable and hardly changed, whereas business processes are continually improved.

SAP EAD supports three notations for business process modelling:

- Value Flow Notation

- Business Process Model and Notation (BPMN)

- Value Stream Mapping

125

Each notation breaks down the business processes to different levels
of granularity. Please note that in SAP EAD, the process diagram must be
created before it can be linked to a business process. This book will focus
on Value Flow Notation and Business Process Model and Notation (BPMN)
as they're the most commonly used.

Value Flow Notation

Value Flow Notation depicts how business processes contribute to
generating value in the business. Value Flows identify how value is
generated by the enterprise. Value Flows depict a continuous flow of value
that is ultimately delivered to internal or external customers.

A set of connected business processes are combined to create business
scenarios that can be better understood by stakeholders. In the case of
Value Flows, it is important to note that the business processes are not
necessarily executed in the sequence they are depicted in. Each Value Flow
has specific inputs and outputs that are required to execute the business
processes. A particular business scenario may include activities that fall
within different functional areas; Value Flows encompass these cross-
functional responsibilities. Value Flows themselves can be interrelated
showing how value flows between them.

Figure 5-5 depicts how Business Processes are the building blocks of
Value Flow diagrams.

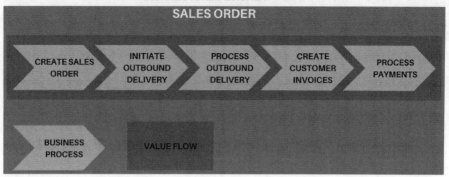

Figure 5-5. *Value Flow diagrams*

Business Process Model and Notation (BPMN)

Business process steps are commonly modelled using Business Process
Model and Notation (BPMN). Business Process Model and Notation
(BPMN) 2.0 is a vendor-independent, standardized, and graphical
notation that encourages collaboration and communication between
business users who must document their processes and developers
seeking to implement them using business execution languages. BPMN
suits instances where the business processes must be understood by
different stakeholders as it can contain various levels of detail to cater to
the interested party. BPMN has the following two complexity levels:

1. **Descriptive** – High-level modelling for beginners

2. **Executable** – Expert-level modelling used for IT
    implementation and includes additional validation
    constraints

As this book is mainly intended for business users and executives, it
focuses on the Descriptive BPMN. Descriptive BPMN is very simple to
use and focuses on the workflow and process steps. Commonly used by
process owners, BPMN 2.0 Descriptive is aimed at business users and

contains a subset of the BPMN 2.0 objects suitable for business process design and analysis. Descriptive process diagrams focus on the sequence flow in a single process, and collaboration diagrams, which include two or more pools, with messages passing between them.

See 5.1 BPMN 2.0 Descriptive diagram – User Guide – SAP Enterprise Architecture Designer – Document Version: 1.0, Page 101.

`https://help.sap.com/doc/1216ca7ff76848a4befadaf6145d04`
`ec/2.0.00/en-us/hana_ea_en.pdf`

As BPMN is the most popular notation, the following sections will explore the individual objects that are used in creating a BPMN process diagram.

Pools

Pools can be businesses, business departments, or business roles. Pools are segmented into "swim lanes" that are sub-entities within these businesses, business departments, or business roles. BPMN process diagrams have one or more pools, with all the other objects placed in the lanes of these pools. Figure 5-6 is a pool containing two lanes and a start event, Sales and Distribution. The green dot represents a start event; this will be looked at later.

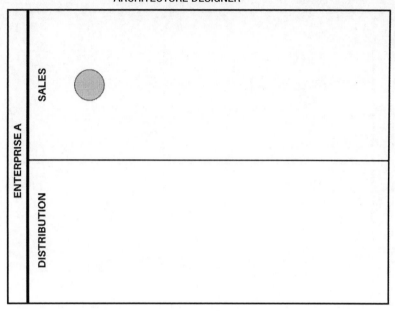

Figure 5-6. *BPMN process diagram containing a pool with two lanes
and a start event*

Pools can be vertical (top to bottom) or horizontal (left to right). SAP
EAD accommodates both.

In Figure 5-7, we see that BPMN process diagrams may contain a
second pool to represent a partner, such as a customer or supplier with
whom the enterprise conducts business activities.

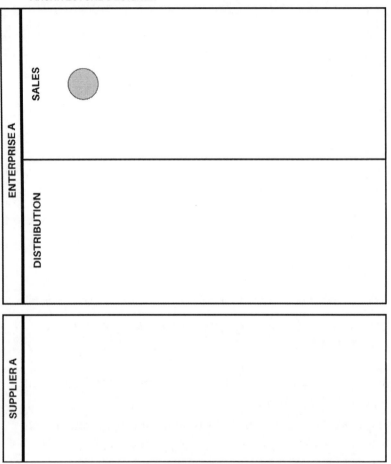

Figure 5-7. *BPMN diagram containing a second pool (supplier)*

SAP EAD allows you to name objects according to your specific
enterprise. However, it is important to remember that the name of the
object should communicate its purpose to business users.

Start Events

A business process is triggered by a start event. There are three kinds of
start events:

Undefined start event – The process begins without any specific triggering event.

Message start event – A message is received that triggers the start of the process, for example, an account inquiry.

Timer start event – The process is triggered at a specific date or time.

See Table 43 Descriptive diagram – User Guide – SAP Enterprise Architecture Designer – Document Version: 1.0, Page 101.

https://help.sap.com/doc/1216ca7ff76848a4befadaf6145d04 ec/2.0.00/en-us/hana_ea_en.pdf

End Events

As highlighted, a business process is triggered by a start event and concludes with one or more end events.

Standard end event – The process ends when all of the tasks are completed.

Message end event – A final message is sent out that terminates the process such as an account statement.

Terminate end event – Parallel tasks are all ended at the same time once one of them reaches the terminate end event.

See Table 43 Descriptive diagram – User Guide – SAP Enterprise Architecture Designer – Document Version: 1.0, Page 102.

https://help.sap.com/doc/1216ca7ff76848a4befadaf6145d04 ec/2.0.00/en-us/hana_ea_en.pdf

Tasks

Tasks are the activities that are carried out during a business process such as raising a purchase order.

There are four types of tasks:

Standard task – Can be used for any kind of activity.

Service task – An activity carried out without any human intervention, for instance, by a web application.

User task – An activity carried out by a human interacting with a software application.

Call activity – This activity calls a preexisting globally defined process such as a user sign-in process and reuses it in multiple processes.

See Table 48 Tasks (BPMN Descriptive) – User Guide – SAP Enterprise Architecture Designer – Document Version: 1.0, Page 106.

`https://help.sap.com/doc/1216ca7ff76848a4befadaf6145d04`
`ec/2.0.00/en-us/hana_ea_en.pdf`

Tasks can further be broken down into subtasks. For example, the user sign-in task can be broken down into the subtasks Enter User Name and Enter Password, as shown in Figure 5-8.

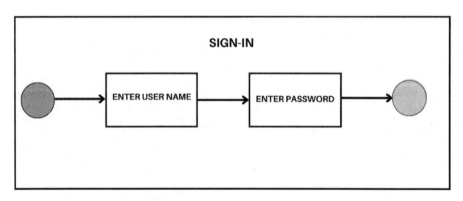

Figure 5-8. *Subtasks in SAP EAD*

Gateways

Gateways dictate the sequence flow of the process including splitting and merging the flow. This can be used to depict scenarios that require conditions to be met before proceeding, decision making and parallel processes.

Exclusive gateway – Only one path is performed, depending on the condition.

Parallel gateway – All outgoing sequence flows are performed simultaneously.

New objects can be added along a new path, and the path should depart from a different corner of the gateway symbol.

To specify a condition on a path connecting the gateway to an object, select the path and enter an appropriate value in the Condition Alias field in the Properties panel. The value is displayed in the diagram on the sequence flow near to the gateway.

You should add a condition to all sequence flows leaving the gateway.

Gateways can be used to merge sequence flows when two or more parallel or exclusive sequence flows come together again to continue the process:

Exclusive gateway – Waits for one incoming path to complete before continuing

Parallel gateway – Waits for all incoming path to complete before continuing

See 5.1.4 Gateways (BPMN Descriptive) – User Guide – SAP Enterprise Architecture Designer – Document Version: 1.0, Pages 108–111.

```
https://help.sap.com/doc/1216ca7ff76848a4befadaf6145d04
ec/2.0.00/en-us/hana_ea_en.pdf
```

Data Objects

Data consumed in the business processes is depicted by data objects. There are two types of data objects:

Data object – Information used in the process

Data store – A data source (database, physical documents) from which the activity can read or to which it can write data and which persists beyond the lifetime of the execution of the process

See Table 53 Data (BPMN Descriptive) – User Guide – SAP Enterprise
Architecture Designer – Document Version: 1.0, Page 112, which you
can find at

https://help.sap.com/doc/1216ca7ff76848a4befadaf6145d04
ec/2.0.00/en-us/hana_ea_en.pdf

Figure 5-9 shows a task reading from a data object or data store.

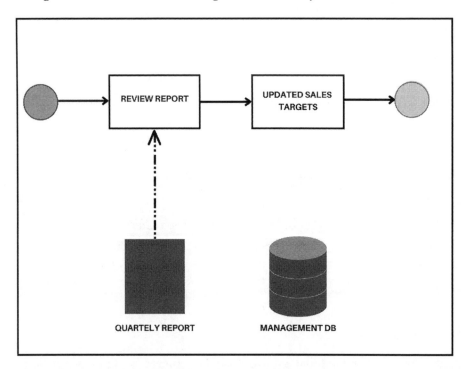

Figure 5-9. *Task reading from a data object or data store*

Figure 5-10 illustrates a task (or other objects) writing to a data object
or data store.

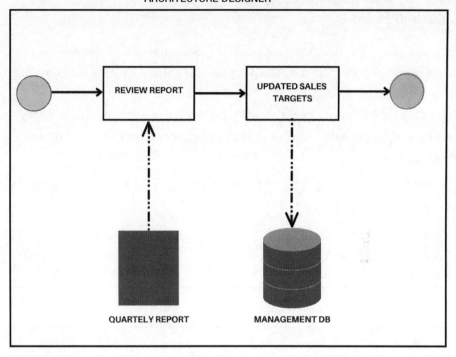

Figure 5-10. *Task (or other objects) writing to a data object or
data store*

Data associations cannot be made between objects in different pools,
that is, linking an object inside the pool with a data object outside of that
specific pool.

Sequence Flows (Paths)

Sequence flows link the elements in a business process and represent their
order of execution. Sequence flows are depicted through a solid line with
an arrow showing the direction of the sequence.

Message Flows

Message flows link two separate pools (or elements in two separate
pools) and via dotted lines with an arrow that shows the direction that the
message is being sent in.

In Figure 5-11, note how the flows between tasks in a single pool are
solid line sequence flows, while the flows between pools are dotted line
message flows.

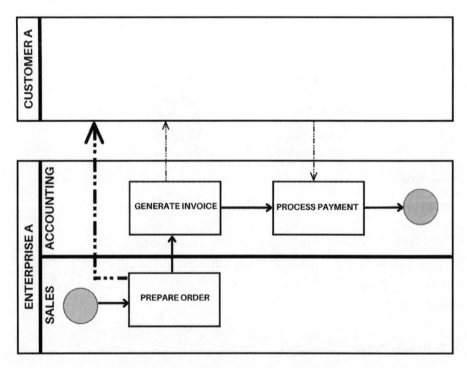

Figure 5-11. *Distinguishing between sequence flows and*
message flows

For more information, see 5.1.6 Sequence and Message Flows (BPMN
Descriptive) – User Guide – SAP Enterprise Architecture Designer –
Document Version: 1.0, Page 114, which you can find at

```
https://help.sap.com/doc/1216ca7ff76848a4befadaf6145d04
ec/2.0.00/en-us/hana_ea_en.pdf
```

The Executable BPMN will include all of the preceding elements and more elements to allow for the more detailed modelling required for IT implementation. For instance, the Descriptive BPMN has the following tasks as mentioned earlier:

- Normal task

- Service task

- User task

- Subprocess

- Call activity

In contrast, the Executable BPMN has the following tasks to accommodate greater detail:

- Normal task

- Service task

- Script task

- User task

- Manual task

- Business rule task

- Send task

- Subprocess

- Call activity

SAP EAD supports collaboration by allowing users to import and export BPMN models.

137

Importing and Exporting Business Processes with SAP Enterprise Designer

SAP EAD allows users to import BPMN models from various sources including

- BPMN template files from BPMN.org

- CSV format

- SAP Solution Manager 7.2

BPMN.org is a BPMN resource for Business Process Model and Notation that includes downloadable BPMN model templates. After downloading a BPMN model template, you can import it directly into SAP EAD using the "Import BPMN2 File" option in the menu.

SAP Solution Manager is an environment for managing and monitoring business processes. SAP EAD can import SAP Solution Manager 7.2 process diagrams. You can share and comment on these business process diagrams, link their objects to objects in other models, and include them in impact analysis. You can edit process diagrams imported from SAP Solution Manager, create new diagrams inside the processes you have imported, and export your changes back to Solution Manager. SAP Solution Manager and EA Designer can exchange BPMN models SAP Solution Manager provides an API that is used by EA Designer to exchange the data interface is bidirectional to ensure data lifecycle.

Exporting a BPMN Model

There are instances where you may wish to export your models for collaboration or review. This collaboration and review may be carried out by

- Team members using a different server (for large organizations)

- External partners

Use the SAP EAD repository browser to navigate to the model you want to export.

Click tools and select Export to Repository Zip File.

A zip file is exported that contains the model saved as a .json file that can be used to transfer models from one repository to another.

Other SAP EAD users can import the zip file as it is and import the model into SAP EAD.

See 5.2.10 Importing and Exporting BPMN 2.0 Files SAP – User Guide – SAP Enterprise Architecture Designer – Document Version: 1.0, Pages 127–129.

https://help.sap.com/doc/1216ca7ff76848a4befadaf6145d04ec/2.0.00/en-us/hana_ea_en.pdf

Summary

Business architecture forms the foundation of all other architecture domains. SAP EAD offers the tools to create and define all elements required to form a robust business architecture that sets the tone for IT and business alignment. SAP EAD allows you to list and prioritize your business capabilities via heatmapping. This supports investment decisions, and the enterprise can also identify gaps that may exist in how they do business.

Once capabilities are documented, SAP EAD provides the tools for mapping the business processes that lead to the realization of those business capabilities. SAP EAD supports the Value Flow Notation and the popular Business Process Model and Notation (BPMN) to model diagrams suitable for different stakeholders. Value Flows clearly depict the value-

generating business processes an enterprise conducts – this is critical
for any executive or manager in terms of identifying areas of operational
improvement. Value Flows are purely business views.

BPMN process diagrams come in two variations/types, namely, the
Descriptive and Executable. Descriptive versions are made for occasional,
nontechnical business users that require a high-level understanding of
the business processes. Executable versions are more detailed and are
utilized by expert modellers mainly for IT implementation. SAP EAD
accommodates both versions by segmenting the functionality available
between the two with the Executable version offering more task types and
modelling elements.

Lastly, we looked at SAP EAD's capabilities in regard to importing
and exporting business process diagrams. SAP EAD can import and
export BPMN files and zip files (containing a .json file of the model)
which enables time-saving, template-based modelling and supports
collaboration between members of your enterprise or with external
partners.

CHAPTER 6

Developing Information Architecture Using SAP EAD

Defining business processes and capabilities by developing a business architecture helps articulate what data services, data sources, and data types are required to support those business processes and capabilities. Knowing which business functions utilize information; where data is created, consumed, and stored; and which technology components store and manipulate the information is crucial to achieving business objectives.

An enterprise has to define the data sources and data types required to support its business activities in a way that can be understood by all relevant stakeholders. All of the important information processing needs of the enterprise must be captured in the information architecture. A well-developed Information Architecture will enable the enterprise to identify any shortfalls in data services such as the wrong type of data being delivered or data not being in the right location.

It is important to note that Information Architecture is not necessarily about designing logical or physical storage systems though relationships

© Sheunopa Chalmers Musukutwa 2022
S. C. Musukutwa, *SAP Enterprise Architecture*, https://doi.org/10.1007/978-1-4842-8575-6_6

with existing systems may be depicted. The goal of Information Architecture is to define the data entities relevant to the enterprise.

SAP Enterprise Architecture Designer provides your enterprise with the capabilities to model your information architecture from a database-independent Conceptual Data Model, a Physical Data Model, and modelling data movement between your data locations. SAP EAD is a useful tool for capturing, analyzing, and presenting your enterprise's information landscape, data requirements, and relationships using industry standard notations, models, principles, and techniques.

Business processes consume and produce data. As introduced in Chapter 1, Information Architecture comprises rules, standards, policies, and models that determine the nature of the data to be collected, the manner in which it is stored and leveraged by your enterprise. A data architecture describes the data structure utilized by your enterprise's applications and business processes. This chapter explores how SAP Enterprise Architecture Designer can be utilized in developing your enterprise's Information Architecture. This chapter will close by demonstrating how SAP accommodates other vendors' databases through its reverse-engineering capabilities.

Conceptual Data Model

The Conceptual Data Model is a business-driven description of an enterprise's data structures and assets. For example, in an ecommerce business, a sales order is executed by a customer; the customer has a name, address, and other data required to complete the sales order. The information that is required for the sales order process and all other business processes in the enterprise should be identified through a Conceptual Data Model. These items are later transformed into a format that a specific database can process.

The conceptual data model is used to design and analyze the information needs from a business perspective and help you identify the principal entities to be represented, their attributes, and the relationships between them. The visually driven Conceptual Data Modelling with the SAP EAD is database independent, supports many-to-many relationships, and supports inheritance.

The modelling objects available in SAP EAD are

- Entities

- Attributes (data items)

- Relationships

- Structured data types

- Associations

- Inheritances

To reiterate, the Conceptual Data Model is about identifying what information the enterprise's day-to-day business processes need and how to represent that information in a manner that can be understood by stakeholders.

See 6.1 Conceptual Data – User Guide – SAP Enterprise Architecture Designer – Document Version: 1.0.4, Page 158.

`https://help.sap.com/doc/1216ca7ff76848a4befadaf6145d04`
`ec/1.0.04/en-US/ea_designer_en.pdf`

Entities

A business has objects it would like to store information about such as a person/customer, sales orders, sales person, etc. Those objects are represented as entities. The information that is used to describe the entity (e.g., "First Name" or "Title" of the person entity) is represented by attributes or data items. The entity stores all of these attributes as a data set.

See 6.1.1 Entities – User Guide – SAP Enterprise Architecture
Designer – Document Version: 1.0.4, Page 159.

https://help.sap.com/doc/1216ca7ff76848a4befadaf6145d04
ec/1.0.04/en-US/ea_designer_en.pdf

Attributes (Data Items)

Data items or attributes represent the characteristics of an entity. What
does the business need to know about the person? Their first name,
telephone number, address, etc.

See 6.1.1.1 Attributes – User Guide – SAP Enterprise Architecture
Designer – Document Version: 1.0.4, Page 160.

https://help.sap.com/doc/1216ca7ff76848a4befadaf6145d04
ec/1.0.04/en-US/ea_designer_en.pdf

SAP EAD allows you to either create the attributes of an entity
directly in the entity or to create separate data items that can be reused as
attributes in different entities. You can define a data item such as "name"
of a person with a variable data type and character limit of 20. You can
then link any entity's name attributes to this data item rather than creating
a new name attribute for that entity.

Structured Data Types

Structured data types better define an attribute through a combination of
data items. For example, money can be better described by two data items,
its value and its currency. A structured data type called "amount" that
consists of value and currency can be created for this purpose.

Identifiers (Index)

An entity will also consist of an index that represents a unique identifier of each data set of attributes. This essentially identifies each occurrence of the entity. For example, for the person entity, the person ID can be an index that uniquely identifies each person and their associated attributes (dataset) such as first name, address, telephone number, etc.

Relationships

Relationships depict how two entities relate to each other. In particular, it specifies the number of instances of each entity that can or must participate in the relationship.

– One-to-many relationship

An Account Exec may handle one or more accounts. An account may only be managed by one Account Exec.

– One-to-many dependent relationship

Each order may contain one or more order lines. Each order is contained by exactly one order. The triangle signifies the dependency.

The fundamental difference between the one-to-many relationship and the one-to-many dependent relationship is the fundamental question, could or must?

In the one-to-many relationship, the first entity **could** have one or more items, whereas in the one-to-many dependent relationship, the first entity **must** have one or more items.

– Many-to-many relationship (M-to-N relations)

Each shipment may have one or more products. Each product may be in one or more shipments.

See 6.1.2 Relationships – User Guide – SAP Enterprise Architecture Designer – Document Version: 1.0.4, Page 163.

```
https://help.sap.com/doc/1216ca7ff76848a4befadaf6145d04
ec/1.0.04/en-US/ea_designer_en.pdf
```

Inheritances

Inheritance specifies a parent-child-like relationship between entities. The parent holds attributes that are common to multiple entities, whereas the child only holds attributes specific to it.

See 6.1.3 Inheritances – User Guide – SAP Enterprise Architecture Designer – Document Version: 1.0.4, Page 166.

```
https://help.sap.com/doc/1216ca7ff76848a4befadaf6145d04
ec/1.0.04/en-US/ea_designer_en.pdf
```

Once the Conceptual Data Model (CDM) has been developed, SAP EAD can generate a Physical Data Model based on the CDM. If there are any changes to that CDM, you can regenerate to that same Physical Data Model to reflect those changes. Changes will go through unless they conflict with changes made on the PDM's side. There is an opportunity to review changes before regenerating the PDM.

The inheritances generated are controlled by inheritance options which determine which tables are generated among the parents and children of your inheritances.

See 6.1.7 Generating a CDM to a PDM – User Guide – SAP Enterprise Architecture Designer – Document Version: 1.0.4, Page 171, available at

```
https://help.sap.com/doc/1216ca7ff76848a4befadaf6145d04
ec/1.0.04/en-US/ea_designer_en.pdf
```

Domains

SAP EAD also includes the concept of domains. Domains are standard data types for a data model that ensure consistency on a data model once it is transformed into a physical data model or during an extract, transform, and load process. This is particularly handy when using the same data model on different databases that may interpret it differently. A name attribute of 60 characters may be transformed into a name attribute of 20 characters in another database.

The Conceptual Data Model is an efficient way to structure your thoughts and describe the important information in your business and is useful for communicating ideas to various stakeholders.

Generating a Physical Data Model

A Physical Data Model (PDM) is a database-specific model that represents the actual relationships and structure of data within the database. A physical data model can be used to generate Data Definition Language statements (DDL) which can then be deployed to a database.

There are three ways to generate a Physical Data Model in HANA 2.0:

1. Generate from existing Conceptual Data Model.

2. Reverse-engineer an existing DBMS into a Physical Data Model.

3. Create a new Physical Data Model.

Generate a Physical Data Model from an Existing Conceptual Data Model

All of the objects defined in the CDM are transformed into objects applicable to the PDM.

Whereas in the CDM there are attributes, entities, and relationships, these objects are transformed into columns, tables, and references, respectively. Other supported objects are

- View with column and view index

- User, schema, group, role

- Domain, abstract data type, sequences

The PDM is similar to the CDM, but there are some differences. The PDM includes arrows that now represent what were relationships in the CDM but are now references in the PDM.

Generating a Physical Data Model from an Existing Database Schema

SAP supports the following databases and data sources for reengineering and generation in SAP HANA:

- SAP HANA 2.0 Deployment Infrastructure (HDI)

- SAP HANA 2.0 Database

- SAP SQL Anywhere 17

- Oracle 12c

- Microsoft SQL Server 2016

- IBM DB2 v11 for z/OS

- Teradata 15

148

The reverse-engineering database selection page in SAP EAD has a left panel that shows available database schemas to choose from. Selecting a schema reveals the objects available for selection when generating a PDM. Objects can be selected from multiple schemas.

SAP EAD shows the selected objects and automatically includes default items in your model.

There are instances when there may be a need to generate or regenerate into an existing PDM. In this situation, a "merge screen" will appear for comparing the new PDM's selected objects and the existing PDM's objects. It lists all differences and includes radio buttons and checkboxes to select the changes to take place and to which objects. SAP EAD utilizes graphic colors to represent areas where changes will take place.

Furthermore, SAP EAD includes the capabilities to make manual changes to the model before generating it. SAP EAD also automatically migrates the primary key in the process.

While all of this is taking place, on the bottom right of the screen, SAP EAD compiles the Data Definition Language (DDL) statements for the generation of this model.

These DDL statements can be saved as files, on Git or directly to the database. Select the "Save" tab on the top-right corner and select "Generate Database." If you choose to generate the PDM directly to the database, you will get the option to select which objects you would like to generate.

There is an option of previewing the DDL statements before saving them.

Once the model has been generated, SAP EAD provides functionality to verify that the model is working. Additionally, SAP EAD also runs its own rule-based checks to identify any issues with the model and flags them graphically.

It is important to note that the SAP HANA function of virtual or proxy tables can be depicted in SAP EAD. Virtual tables are tables in another database that can be accessed remotely.

If you choose to generate the PDM directly to the database, you will get the option to select which objects you would like to generate.

Data Movement Model

Most enterprises have information stored in different databases and applications. A Data Movement Model (DMM) provides insight into the movement of this data between different points and how it is transformed along the way. A DMM depicts the flow and transformation of data from source models to target models.

For more information, see 6.4 Data Movement – User Guide – SAP Enterprise Architecture Designer – Document Version: 1.0.4, Page 297, available at

`https://help.sap.com/doc/1216ca7ff76848a4befadaf6145d04`
`ec/1.0.04/en-US/ea_designer_en.pdf`

Data movement modelling results in a flow definition that can be used:

- As a guide for an ETL tool implementation

- To generate FlowGraph in SAP HANA's own ETL tool, Smart Data Integration (SDI)

A new Data Movement Model can be created, or an existing FlowGraph can be edited through reverse-engineering a FlowGraph file.

Creating a New DMM Diagram

You can generate conceptual objects into the elements of a Physical Data Model as shown in Table 6-1. Furthermore, you can create a DMM using the constructing elements in Table 6-2.

Table 6-1. *Generating Conceptual Objects into a Physical Data Model*

Conceptual Objects	Standard DBMS	SAP HANA 2.0 HDI
Entities	Tables	Entities
Attributes	Columns	Elements
Identifiers	Keys	Elements with *Key* property set to true
Relationships	References	Associations
Inheritances	Options control generation of parent and child tables	Options control generation of parent and child entities
Domains	Domains	Simple types
Structured types	Abstract data types	Structured types
Data items	[Not generated]	[Not generated]

Table 6-2. *DMM Constructing Elements*

Constructing Element	Use
Data input	Represents a source of data in a data transformation diagram and is linked to a database, an XML document, a web service, or a flat file
Data output	Represents a target destination to load data in a data transformation diagram and is linked to a database, an XML document, or a flat file
Data join	Performs a join on two or more input flows and combines them

(*Continued*)

Table 6-2. *(Continued)*

Constructing Element	Use
Data query	Executes an SQL query against a database for each row of the input flow to transform it and create a new data flow. Data from the input flow can be used as a parameter
Data filter	Filters incoming rows using SQL criteria
Data union	Combines two or more identical input flows into a single output flow
Data flow	Conveys data between steps in a data transformation diagram
Data aggregation	Aggregates incoming data using functions such as Avg, Min, Max
Data projection	Responsible for data transformations such as reordering or deleting columns
Data sort	Sorts incoming rows by one or more data structure columns
Data split	Duplicates a simple input data flow into two or more identical output data flows
Transform	Performs various simple transformations such as joins, sorts, filters, and aggregations

There are four steps to designing the DMM:

1. Select the data input constructing element to specify the data source. Thereafter, assign an existing entity from an SAP EAD model to the database input element as the data source.

2. It is possible to manually map the source elements (attributes) with the target elements by adding the data projection element and defining the mapping.

3. Any required filtering can be added to the incoming data with the filter element by defining filtering criteria in SQL.

4. Lastly, add a data output element and assign an existing SAP EAD model object.

Using SAP EAD, we can now generate the FlowGraph file that can be utilized by developers in Web IDE for SAP HANA. This is a simplified example that clearly shows how DMM can be developed from a given SAP EAD model and used to generate a FlowGraph useful for implementing an extract, transform, and load (ETL) tool.

For more information, see 6.4 Data Movement – User Guide – SAP Enterprise Architecture Designer – Document Version: 1.0.4, Page 298, available at

https://help.sap.com/doc/1216ca7ff76848a4befadaf6145d04
ec/1.0.04/en-US/ea_designer_en.pdf

Reverse-Engineering a FlowGraph File

As mentioned, a FlowGraph file can be reengineered from SAP Web IDE for SAP HANA. Simply select the option "reverse engineer flowgraph file" in the menu and navigate to the FlowGraph file.

For further information, see 6.4.4 Reverse-Engineering – User Guide – SAP Enterprise Architecture Designer – Document Version: 1.0.4, Page 297, available at

https://help.sap.com/doc/1216ca7ff76848a4befadaf6145d04
ec/1.0.04/en-US/ea_designer_en.pdf

Non-SAP Databases and Data Models

SAP designs all of its products to be as vendor-agnostic as possible. As highlighted earlier, SAP can reverse-engineer the following databases for analysis and mapping back into a HANA database:

- IBM DB2 Version 11 for z/OS

- Microsoft SQL Server 2016

- Oracle 12c

- SAP HANA 2.0 Database

- SAP HANA 2.0 HDI

- SAP SQL Anywhere 17

- Teradata Version 15

Reverse-Engineering an Existing Schema

1. Click Create New Diagram to start creating a new model in SAP EAD.

2. In the menu, select "Reverse Engineer Database."

3. You can either connect to the database by specifying connection details or upload a DDL statement file.

4. The SAP EAD Reverse Engineering selection page allows you to select the elements you would like to reverse-engineer.

The physical data model is then generated including the selected objects. This data model can now be regenerated for any other database.

This process transforms any physical characteristics that don't match between the PDM and the target database. For example, the PDM may have a data type called "VarChar2," whereas the target database calls the same data type "VarChar." This process is similar to the process shown on how to generate objects from a PDM in a database using the same merge view that compares the differences between the PDM and the target database model.

Summary

This chapter sought to share some of the Information Architecture capabilities of SAP EAD. Every business has information it requires to collect, consume, and produce in order to effectively execute its business processes. SAP EAD helps to model this information in a manner that can be communicated to multiple stakeholders.

Information Architecture starts with modelling the Conceptual Data Model which captures all of the information requirements and types independent of any database. SAP EAD provides the functionality to efficiently model and verify the Conceptual Data Model and use it to generate a Physical Data Model. Any changes to the original Conceptual Data Model can be regenerated into the Physical Data Model and update it.

The Physical Data Model is database specific and hence more detailed than the Conceptual Data Model. The Physical Data Model can also be reverse-engineered from an existing database and regenerated for another database using SAP EAD. SAP EAD also allows you to create a completely new Physical Data Model.

For the purposes of ETL (extract, transform, and load), a Data Movement Model can be utilized to depict the flow of data from and to different data stores and applications. The Data Movement Model can also be used to generate a FlowGraph that can be used with SAP HANA's ETL tool "SDI" to transform data from a remote source into SAP HANA.

Lastly, SAP accommodates other vendors' databases through the reverse-engineering functionality. You can reverse-engineer the database in SAP EAD producing a physical data model that can then be generated into another database model if need be.

CHAPTER 7

Developing Infrastructure Architecture Using SAP EAD

Infrastructure Architecture refers to the underlying infrastructure required to run the business. It describes the logical software and hardware capabilities that are required to support the deployment of business, data, and application services. This chapter explores how SAP Enterprise Architecture Designer helps you to document, analyze, and visualize your enterprise's system landscape.

In SAP EAD, Infrastructure Architecture is broken down into Landscape and System Architecture. Landscape and System Architecture comprises three facets:

-   Application Architecture Modelling

-   Service Modelling

-   Infrastructure Architecture Modelling

© Sheunopa Chalmers Musukutwa 2022
S. C. Musukutwa, *SAP Enterprise Architecture*, https://doi.org/10.1007/978-1-4842-8575-6_7

A model is the logical representation implementation of an idea of how things work together in a particular domain. Similar to the other architecture domains, SAP EAD takes an object-driven approach to modelling your infrastructure architecture. For instance, Application Architecture Modelling represents assets such as databases, forms, and documents as objects you can drag and drop into your model. The significant difference is that whereas other domains largely dealt with logical objects, Infrastructure Architecture includes physical assets such as servers, data centers, and network nodes.

This chapter explores how SAP EAD enables the business to model their technological infrastructure in a way that not only accurately depicts their environment but also shows the relationships between the objects in it. This supports the planning process and change management as the business will be able to understand the impact of any change not only on the object that is the subject of the change but also on the objects that have relationships with it.

Ultimately, this last stage of Enterprise Architecture using SAP EAD will allow for the confident completion of the process of business and IT alignment. This is accomplished by linking the business services modelled during business architecture to the applications and physical infrastructure that is responsible for supporting them.

This chapter begins by looking at Application Architecture Modelling which visualizes the relationships between various IT infrastructure components.

Application Architecture Modelling

Application Architecture Modelling visualizes the relationships between the objects within your IT infrastructure. These objects are grouped together and represent an application which serves a particular purpose within the enterprise. For instance, an application may provide functionality that is key in delivering a business service such as checking a bank account balance. SAP EAD utilizes the following Application Architecture objects as the building blocks for modelling your software assets:

- Application

- System

- Database

- ETL jobs

- Architecture areas

- Components

The following sections will expand on these components.

Application

Applications can contain subapplications, forms, and subcomponents. SAP EAD allows you to enter specific details about the application under the "info tab" such as its programming language, type of application, operating system, etc. SAP EAD ensures that all relevant application information is easily accessible, including tabs for the application's children and dependencies. This gives a view of the objects that are impacted by any changes to the application. The children are the components contained within the application. Dependencies refer to objects that the application depends on, for instance, a database that the application stores or retrieves data from.

For more information, see 3.6 Application Architecture Modeling – User Guide – SAP Enterprise Architecture Designer – Document Version: 1.0, Page 73, available at

```
https://help.sap.com/doc/1216ca7ff76848a4befadaf6145d04
ec/2.0.00/en-us/hana_ea_en.pdf
```

Applications can be linked with application services, components, and systems.

System Modelling

A system represents the entire environment that an application functions in and can contain subsystems, applications and application services, databases, ETL jobs, documents, components, and forms. The system object also has information about its children and dependencies.

For more information, see 3.6.1 Systems and Applications (EAM) – User Guide – SAP Enterprise Architecture Designer – Document Version: 1.0, Page 75, available at

https://help.sap.com/doc/1216ca7ff76848a4befadaf6145d04ec/2.0.00/en-us/hana_ea_en.pdf

Database

Database objects represent a data store. The database object can be linked to a physical data model through the dependencies tab by adding a physical data model under "Source Models."

The SAP EAD database modelling module supports the following database types:

- Data warehouse
- Data mart
- Multidimensional data warehouse
- OLTP database
- Virtual database

For more information, see 3.6.2 Databases (EAM) – User Guide – SAP Enterprise Architecture Designer – Document Version: 1.0, Page 76, available at

```
https://help.sap.com/doc/1216ca7ff76848a4befadaf6145d04
ec/2.0.00/en-us/hana_ea_en.pdf
```

ETL Jobs

Extract, transform, and load (ETL) jobs are data integration processes that represent movements of data between data stores. These jobs may include the replication (copying), transformation (format conversion), or movement of data. An ETL job object is used to represent these processes in SAP EAD.

For more information, see 3.6.6 ETL Jobs (EAM) – User Guide – SAP Enterprise Architecture Designer – Document Version: 1.0, Page 81, available at

```
https://help.sap.com/doc/1216ca7ff76848a4befadaf6145d04
ec/2.0.00/en-us/hana_ea_en.pdf
```

Architecture Areas

SAP EAD seeks to create architectures that are as detailed as possible in order for them to be understandable to as many stakeholders as possible. SAP EAD utilizes specific objects expressly for structuring and organizing other objects. Architecture areas allow for the logical grouping of objects to speak to a particular audience or for a particular purpose. The objects do not belong to the area but are just grouped in it for the benefit of a specific audience.

Architecture areas can contain sites, processes, applications, and systems, among other objects.

Components

SAP EAD uses components to represent consumable parts of an application which can be used to implement a service or an application. This is to say that a component can exist in an application internally or can exist externally to the application it services.

Other objects in Application Architecture Modelling include

- **Contracts** – Represent agreements between two parties such as a service-level agreement

- **Forms** – Represent a system or application's user interface

- **Documents** – Represent structured information that is produced and consumed by the systems and applications

For more information, see 3.6.3 Components (EAM) – User Guide – SAP Enterprise Architecture Designer – Document Version: 1.0, Page 77, available at

    https://help.sap.com/doc/1216ca7ff76848a4befadaf6145d04
    ec/2.0.00/en-us/hana_ea_en.pdf

Service Modelling

SAP EAD allows you to model the services required and provided by your enterprise. You can build a hierarchical model that shows dependencies between services and truly understand their impact on each other. Each service contains detail such as the type of service it is and the service level required. SAP EAD breaks down its services into business services and application services.

For more information, see 3.6.8 Application and Business Services (EAM) – User Guide – SAP Enterprise Architecture Designer – Document Version: 1.0, Page 83, available at

```
https://help.sap.com/doc/1216ca7ff76848a4befadaf6145d04
ec/2.0.00/en-us/hana_ea_en.pdf
```

Business Services

A business service is a service that the enterprise offers to its customers that supports the activities performed as part of a business capability. A business service captures information such as the business service type (e.g., bookings), quality of service level, security level, and owner.

Application Services

Application services are units of functionality provided by components or applications that can be accessed through service interfaces.

Operations

Business and application services are supported by service operations. Operations are actions that support the delivery of a service. Operations are created via the children tab of the business or application service.

For more information, see 3.6.8.1 Business and Application Service Operations – User Guide – SAP Enterprise Architecture Designer – Document Version: 1.0, Page 85, available at

```
https://help.sap.com/doc/1216ca7ff76848a4befadaf6145d04
ec/2.0.00/en-us/hana_ea_en.pdf
```

Ultimately, all of these objects are brought together to form the big picture and depict the end-to-end process in Figure 7-1.

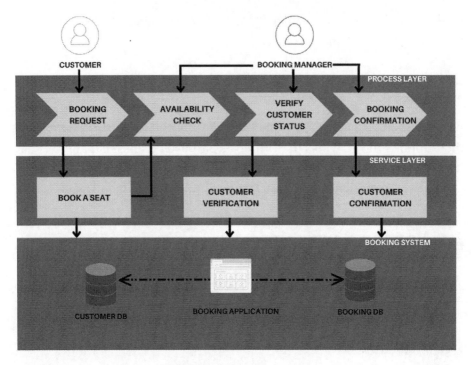

Figure 7-1. *End-to-end booking process*

Figure 7-1 is a booking process for a movie theater and is an illustration of how business services, application services, and operations work together to deliver a movie theater booking service. For instance, the "Book a Seat" business service is supported by the operation "Availability Check" and the booking application.

Infrastructure Architecture Modelling

Whereas Application Modelling and Service Modelling dealt with software assets, we will now explore the physical infrastructure that supports your activities. SAP EAD supports the modelling of the physical infrastructure that supports your activities. SAP EAD breaks down an enterprise's infrastructure into Organizational Infrastructure and Infrastructure

Architecture. Organizational Infrastructure includes objects such as site, organizational unit, person, and role. Infrastructure Architecture includes networks, hardware server, mobile devices, etc. Organizational Infrastructure and Infrastructure Architecture can be used for location and data center modelling.

Organizational Infrastructure Modelling

Organizational Infrastructure Modelling is about capturing how the business organizes its people and physical infrastructure to perform the work and to achieve its goals and objectives. SAP EAD includes functionality to model sites and organizational units.

Site

Similar to the architecture areas introduced earlier in the chapter, a site acts as a container to structure other objects including other sites (nested sites), networks, servers, organizational units, etc. Figure 7-2 shows a sample site with a server room that contains two servers. Server 1 hosts the customer database, and server 2 hosts the booking database.

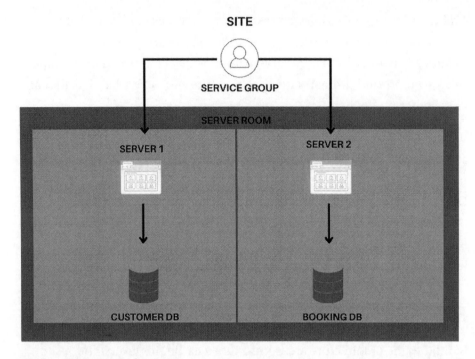

Figure 7-2. Sample site

For more information, see 3.4.1 Sites (EAM) – User Guide – SAP Enterprise Architecture Designer – Document Version: 1.0, Page 63, available at

https://help.sap.com/doc/1216ca7ff76848a4befadaf6145d04 ec/2.0.00/en-us/hana_ea_en.pdf

Each object within a site has its own individual properties that can be specified such as the Database Management System (DBMS) on a database object. Each site has various properties such as name, address, systems, etc. Sites can be nested within each other to form a hierarchy that can detail exactly what room or even rack a hardware object is located in.

Organizational Unit

An organizational unit is an object that represents a department or group and can itself contain other subunits. Organizational units are useful when assigning particular personnel to specific sites/data centers or assigning ownership/responsibility for infrastructure assets. Organizational units can be represented as persons or roles, as shown in Figure 7-3.

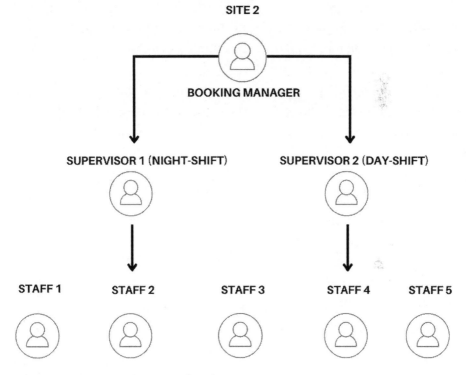

Figure 7-3. *Organizational unit*

For more information, see 3.4.2 Organization Units (EAM) – User Guide – SAP Enterprise Architecture Designer – Document Version: 1.0, Page 65, available at

https://help.sap.com/doc/1216ca7ff76848a4befadaf6145d04
ec/2.0.00/en-us/hana_ea_en.pdf

Infrastructure Architecture Modelling

SAP EAD supports the modelling of the enterprise's technology infrastructure to provide enterprise-wide insight into the networks, servers, and workstations in the technological environment.

Network

Networks enable computer devices to communicate with each other. The network object can represent the communication between both software and hardware assets on the network.

All other objects, such as servers, workstations, mobile devices, etc., reside within the network and can be represented accordingly. SAP EAD accommodates the following objects:

- Hardware server

- Software server

- Workstation

- Mobile device

- Network node

SAP EAD can also model machine-in-machine environments such as virtual machines and cluster servers by specifying the relevant property to "Virtual" or "Cluster Server"; see Figure 7-4.

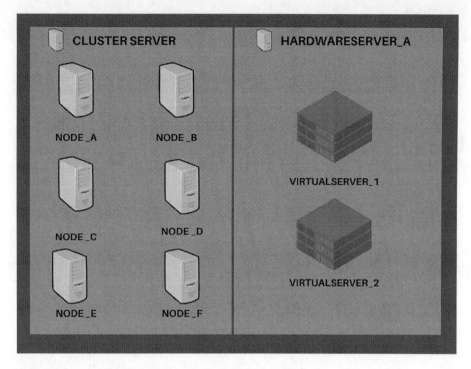

Figure 7-4. *Virtual server and cluster server*

This concludes our discussion on the modelling aspects of developing an Infrastructure Architecture. After developing your models, it is important to leverage their interconnectedness. It is this interconnectedness that provides a truly enterprise-wide view of the business and enables better planning, change management, and control. The potential impact of a change in one domain can be analyzed from the perspective of all other domains.

For more information, see 3.7.1 Servers, Workstations, Mobile Devices, and Network Nodes (EAM) – User Guide – SAP Enterprise Architecture Designer – Document Version: 1.0, Page 86, available at

`https://help.sap.com/doc/1216ca7ff76848a4befadaf6145d04`
`ec/2.0.00/en-us/hana_ea_en.pdf`

See 3.7.2 Networks (EAM) – User Guide – SAP Enterprise Architecture Designer – Document Version: 1.0, Page 89.

```
https://help.sap.com/doc/1216ca7ff76848a4befadaf6145d04
ec/2.0.00/en-us/hana_ea_en.pdf
```

Impact and Lineage Analysis

One of the advantages of having a central repository for all models is that all of the objects are linked. This forms the foundation for Impact and Lineage (Origin) Analysis. SAP EAD provides a graphical representation of these links to gain insight into the relationships between objects and the impact of any potential changes.

Impact Analysis can be conducted by clicking the specific object you want to analyze. A context menu will appear; select Impact Analysis.

The Impact and Lineage Analysis is generated in real time with the impacted objects being shown on the right of the object being analyzed and the lineage objects being shown on the left of the object being analyzed. You can show the impacts of an object shown among the lineages and vice versa by recentering the analysis on the object by selecting it and clicking the Change Analysis Object tool. It is also possible to modify what types of relationships are displayed by using the Customize Analysis tool.

- Click the object whose analysis you would like to modify.

- Select the Customize Analysis tool.

You will now be able to choose which relationships will be displayed for that object as well as the type of relationship (Impact or Lineage).

A business function, far removed from the initial system, may be selected, and the multiple impact paths that lead to it are automatically highlighted by SAP EAD.

See 1.6 Impact and Lineage Analysis – User Guide – SAP Enterprise Architecture Designer – Document Version: 1.0, Page 41.

```
https://help.sap.com/doc/1216ca7ff76848a4befadaf6145d04
ec/2.0.00/en-us/hana_ea_en.pdf
```

Summary

Ensuring that the enterprise has the right infrastructure to support your business capabilities is critical to achieving business success. SAP EAD allows for the direct mapping of infrastructure assets to the business processes they support to ensure alignment and gain insights into operational efficiency.

SAP EAD models every aspect of the technological landscape in a single repository which in turn gives insight into the relationships between the objects in and across various models. This forms the foundation of Impact and Lineage Analysis which enables the enterprise to plan for change from an informed perspective as you will know the potential impact of any change in the enterprise's environment.

SAP EAD's Infrastructure Architecture is about modelling physical assets such as data centers, server rooms, and server racks. Enterprise Architecture decisions can be made within the context of specific locations that may have different requirements or different business objectives.

This chapter is the final chapter dedicated to SAP EAD exclusively. Enterprise architecture has a lot to do with having a direction (vision, goals) based on an accurate understanding of the enterprise's starting point. SAP EAD helps to clearly articulate the enterprise's current architectural landscape which empowers the decision making and planning process in developing projects that will move the enterprise toward its long-term vision.

CHAPTER 8

Enterprise Architecture Best Practices

Enterprise Architecture is a unique discipline whose origins are still a matter of debate. Many authors routinely bestow that honor on John Zachman's "Zachman Framework" and believe it laid the foundation for EA as a discipline. However, researchers like Svyatoslav Kotusev claim that the origins of EA precede the Zachman Framework and that EA is a product of IBM's Business Systems Planning (BSP). If the origins of a discipline are not clear, there may be a lack of consensus on what it actually is. This has plagued EA over the years. There isn't a universal definition for it. This being the case, one can easily argue that there is consequently no basis for determining how best to practice said discipline.

This book takes the position that the best answer can be found in applying the unique context in which EA will be practiced. There is no one-size-fits-all definition of or best practices for Enterprise Architecture. Professor James Lapalme states that there are three schools of thought on EA, with each having its own definition, scope, and purpose. Firstly, EA may only be concerned with aligning business and IT. Secondly, it may be concerned with architecting the entire enterprise, including IT. Lastly,

© Sheunopa Chalmers Musukutwa 2022
S. C. Musukutwa, *SAP Enterprise Architecture*, https://doi.org/10.1007/978-1-4842-8575-6_8

its concern may be the relationships between the enterprise and its environment. The business should always be clear about why it's choosing EA and what it hopes to achieve.

Best practices are recognized and recommended ways of executing specific processes within your enterprise. For instance, utilizing a SWOT analysis is considered a best practice when determining strategic initiatives. EA does not seek to replace existing best practices but rather assist you in determining how, where, and when they should be used or whether they are delivering the desired outcomes.

When EA is adopted fully, it in itself becomes the final reference for how and when to leverage best practices. It is important to select the most relevant practices in relation to the enterprise and its strategic goals. This is an important factor to highlight because how EA will be practiced will determine what best practices to implement. Enterprises normally face the question of which best practices to adopt. Since an enterprise implements EA according to its unique circumstances, what works for one enterprise may not work for the other. Clearly, the selection of the best practices to take on is one of the more complex parts of EA. The recommendations in this chapter will most likely have to be adjusted to suit your enterprise and address your specific circumstances. For instance, the implementation of EA in your enterprise may require additional change management activities.

Areas such as the infrastructure domain have many best practices to consider; these best practices often address the same area and compete with each other. EA is driven by an organization's strategic goals and desired future state; this provides the context required to determine what best practices should be implemented. It is imperative for EA to be the overarching reference point for the enterprise.

Up until this point, the book has explored what Enterprise Architecture is, and there's been an overview of a tool that can assist in its implementation. This chapter looks at the recommended ways of carrying out that implementation. Best practices are proven ways of implementing

Enterprise Architecture in an efficient way. This chapter provides a general list of best practices which can be implemented, adjusted, or omitted according to the context of the enterprise.

Best Practices for EA

As mentioned, best practices are recognized and recommended ways of executing specific processes within the business. This section goes over the general best practices for EA implementation independent of any specific EA methodology.

Create an EA Charter

An EA charter provides the scope and the reasoning behind your enterprise choosing to implement EA. This is mainly done through detailing the expected benefits of implementing EA and how they will be achieved. The EA charter explicitly identifies all stakeholders and their obligations toward the EA process, acting as an agreement between the EA team and the stakeholders. It clarifies the obligations of the EA team, authority of the EA team, and the relevant decision-making processes.

The EA charter also details the terms of the EA implementation such as what assets will be produced and by when. This is part of defining the criteria for success and allows the EA process to be monitored and evaluated. With that said, what constitutes success will change over time; the EA charter must be reviewed periodically and updated accordingly to ensure its relevance. The EA charter must also cover the risks facing a successful EA implementation ahead of time so that they can be mitigated and monitored.

EA Governance

Governance in the context of EA is the practice of managing and controlling EA on an enterprise level. EA governance generally includes the fundamental aspects of management such as establishing an authoritative hierarchy and sound monitoring processes.

The success or failure of EA depends on the level of oversight, authority, and decision-making power granted to the EA team in discharging their duties. Developing a clear chain of command is a nonnegotiable aspect of EA implementation. Naturally, the EA team's authority should span the entire enterprise and support them in implementing EA across all domains (business, information, infrastructure). It is also recommended to have a wide range of participants that represent different interests as part of the EA team. For instance, leaders from the business domain are less likely to be resistant to change if they have played a part in in defining such a change.

A formal EA Program Management Office should be set up to house the EA team. The EA Program Management Office should be backed by executive support and stakeholder cooperation. The EA Program Management Office should be headed by the Chief Enterprise Architect. The Chief Enterprise Architect must lead collaborative exercises that determine the standards and best practices to be followed throughout the enterprise to achieve the desired future state.

EA governance should not become a burden to the business. It should be "lightweight" and lean on already existing governance procedures within your enterprise. The governance process should clearly identify who is responsible for architecture and compliance decisions as well as the possible disciplinary actions to be faced if need be. One of the goals of EA is to make the business more agile; this includes leaving room to make some exceptions in the governance process.

It is important to note that the EA team should comprise individuals with different skillsets (i.e., modelling, EA governance, EA asset administration, etc.) but common talents (strong communicators, innovators, leadership, etc.).

Business Strategy As a Starting Point

The enterprise's business strategy essentially represents what the business aims to achieve and how it aims to achieve it. It is the business strategy that drives the articulation of the enterprise's desired future state. It is best practice to start by developing a thorough understanding of the enterprise's business strategy because EA exists to support the goals and objectives of the business strategy. Showing how EA supports business strategy plays a key role in winning over the executive of the enterprise who are mainly concerned with the execution of business strategy.

The business strategy also offers a focal point to employ a shared strategy. EA has a lot to do with the enterprise moving in synergy toward a common goal. EA should be founded upon the business strategy to guide the enterprise's decision making, processes, and practices.

Implement a Communications Plan

Each enterprise has its own way of comprehensively disseminating information, but special care should be taken in the case of EA as poor communication tends to be a stumbling block in most instances. The three preceding steps produce assets whose information must be clearly communicated to all stakeholders. It is a best practice to develop a communications plan to share the benefits, scope, and objectives of EA.

Key stakeholders must be identified alongside the targeted messaging that addresses their concerns. The EA team should detail all communication methods that are to be utilized (online meetings, newsletters, etc.) and categorize the most effective communication methods for each stakeholder group. The communications plan should outline specific timelines and responsibilities for communications procedures as well as a feedback process to monitor the execution of the communications plan.

Project-Based Approach

Enterprise Architecture is a continuous process that runs the risk of losing focus and ultimately losing relevance within your enterprise. This can be combated by structuring EA as a continuous set of projects that have a clear start and end point. One of the benefits of a project-based approach is that a project at an enterprise level usually gets assigned an executive sponsor. This is critical to ensure enterprise-wide participation of stakeholders as the support comes from "above." Each project will have its own unique set of deliverables that can be logically sequenced to form a road map toward the desired future state. This has several advantages:

- The enterprise is more flexible and can adapt to change in its environment through projects that address unforeseen circumstances.

- Projects allow for the meeting of short-term goals which helps show the value of EA to stakeholders through improving the value to market cycle.

- Projects allow for a quicker and more consistent feedback cycle.

- The activity planning and resourcing for EA is simplified, better estimated, and better coordinated.

- Each project can have a dedicated specialist project manager which frees the EA team to focus on enterprise-wide duties.

Lastly, structuring the EA as iterative projects allows for agile adoption. At EA's inception, IT projects ran in long cycles spanning years. That has progressively changed with agile methods shortening development time dramatically. Agile methodologies promote collaboration, continuous feedback, and rapid value creation.

Select a Framework

A framework is responsible for structuring the EA process and therefore defines its scope. It depicts the architecture and its subdomains, therefore forming a basis for determining boundaries. These boundaries allow for the clear segmentation of tasks, responsibilities, and stakeholders. Furthermore, it can be used to define the relationships between architectural domains. For instance, it can depict how an information system in the information architecture is critical to business processes in the business architecture. This kind of structuring allows a common enterprise-wide perspective of all the subdomains within the architecture.

EA Frameworks to choose from include

- TOGAF ADM

- Zachman Framework

- Department of Defense Architecture Framework (DoDAF)

- Gartner Enterprise Architecture Framework

Select a Methodology

An EA methodology speaks to the actual execution of the EA process. It provides a detailed step-by-step action plan for creating the EA program, creating the documentation, creating the future and current views of the enterprise, and, lastly, maintaining and utilizing EA assets. EA assets

179

are the resulting products of the EA process including items such as documentation. For instance, the EA charter is one of the products of creating the EA program. Each subdomain presented in the chosen framework has EA assets that will be produced through the execution of the prescribed steps in the methodology. An example would be a network connectivity diagram as part of the EA assets under the infrastructure architecture or a use case diagram under the business architecture.

Central Information Repository

All EA assets must be stored in a central repository and accessible by all relevant parties. An online storage point within the enterprise's internal network is ideal. The repository must be visually presented in a logical way that enables easy navigation for users. Related EA assets should be linked together and consumable from one view.

Define the Future State First

Business strategy by nature speaks to the future of your enterprise. The main goal of EA is to facilitate change toward the achievement of strategic goals. The business would not be implementing EA if the current state of the business was meeting strategic goals. In essence, the only use of defining the current state of the organization is to estimate the effort that is required to accomplish the desired future state, whereas the future state forms the basis of what actually has to be done. Focusing on the future state means the business strategy will stay top of mind as opposed to being bogged down to the current state of the enterprise which is not meeting strategic goals.

Monitor the EA Process

Monitoring the EA process may bring some anxiety to the EA team, but it is a critical best practice. It is important to define metrics at the beginning of the EA process to ensure that EA is delivering business value. The first step to achieving this is through genuinely understanding and taking on all stakeholder concerns. The metrics to monitor EA must align with stakeholder concerns; otherwise, what may seem like success to the EA team theoretically may not mean anything practically. In essence, you are translating stakeholder expectations into tangible and measurable goals.

The EA team should measure and report on progress regularly to ensure that the EA process remains effective. Measuring progress enables your enterprise to make decisions based on reliable data and also allows you to innovatively tackle any issues that may have been exposed through the monitoring process. There is no template of metrics that can apply here because enterprises differ in their goals, strategies, and levels of maturity.

Since EA is a discipline that predominantly addresses how your enterprise will adapt to the future, your EA process itself must evolve. The maturity level of your EA process must be assessed on an annual basis as well as conducting a reevaluation of the measurement metrics in place. What areas of your EA process can be improved to make it more effective? The answers to this question should be translated into an action plan to address these areas for improvement.

Implement a Comprehensive Change Management Strategy

The adoption of EA is a radical change for most enterprises and may initially seem like it is in opposition to the decentralization of power within your enterprise. Managers may feel that the control over their specific domain is being taken away. A comprehensive change management strategy has to be implemented; having a dedicated resource to this effect is considered best practice. Beyond the stakeholders, the enterprise itself may be plagued with siloed processes and systems that have to be done away to enable a truly enterprise-wide approach to be implemented.

The EA process involves an analysis of future and current states of the organization. This may result in exposing the shortcomings of particular departments or individual staff members. Naturally, you can expect some resistance or lack of cooperation. It should be continually communicated that EA is there for the improvement of the organization and therefore will not affect any area that is functioning accordingly.

Articulate and Measure the Value of EA Possible Challenges

Enterprise Architecture can be a resource-heavy endeavor in terms of time, people, and financial resources, to mention a few. These are resources that could be directed to other parts of the enterprise that yield quicker results. The EA team must be cognizant of the fact that they're always in competition with the enterprise's other initiatives. The first way of dealing with this competition is by articulating the value proposition of EA and ensuring that it addresses stakeholder concerns. Secondly, put forward metrics to measure success on a consistent basis so that stakeholders remain informed on progress.

Benefits of Best Practices for EA

This book is not solely about practicing Enterprise Architecture but about practicing Enterprise Architecture efficiently. Following best practices results in business benefits such as

- **Informed decision making** – EA provides an enterprise-wide view of the business that supports business decision making. Decision makers have insight into how a decision in one domain affects other domains.

- **Business and IT alignment** – Implementing best practices ensures that the importance of aligning the EA endeavor with business goals.

- **Agility** – EA is based on frameworks. There may be an inclination to strictly stick to frameworks that may result in the organization becoming rigid. EA best practices ensure that your organization remains flexible and adaptable to change.

- Improved return on investment for projects executed within the EA context. EA best practices allow for the better control and monitoring of projects which leads to saving costs.

EA best practices prescribe steps that ensure that your EA process undergoes continuous improvement on an annual basis. Best practices enable your enterprise to avoid common pitfalls (such as not aligning the EA endeavor with organizational goals) ahead of time because they have been developed from tangible EA experience. These common pitfalls include

EA best practices endorse the adoption of a framework that provides a uniform and enterprise-wide approach of taking on change. This promotes synergy throughout the enterprise which eliminates the old age problem of operating in silos. Lastly, best practices offer a starting point for the level of skills and knowledge required of the EA team.

Things to Avoid

As mentioned in the section "Benefits of Best Practices for EA," there are many common pitfalls you can encounter on your EA journey. Some of them have been listed as follows alongside a short explanation to assist you in being aware of them during the EA process:

Using complex technical jargon – As technical people, the EA team may incorporate complicated jargon that only they understand, overlooking the fact that EA must be understood by all stakeholders to ensure maximum adoption. Utilize plain language to the greatest extent possible.

Neglecting business strategy – Enterprise Architecture is generally seen as a highly technical endeavor, which it is; however, it is a technical endeavor implemented to enable the realization of business goals. Business strategy plays the important role of focusing on the EA process and must always be an overarching consideration. This will also ensure that the EA process remains linked to budgetary concerns.

Being too rigid – Frameworks and methodologies have their rightful place but very rarely will a framework or methodology suit your enterprise perfectly. Frameworks and methodologies serve as a point of reference to promote a common understanding of what is to be accomplished while maintaining a certain level of standards. However, this does not override scenarios where the framework or methodology must be adapted to suit the environmental realities of the organization.

Working in silos – The EA team should never find themselves isolated from stakeholders and neither should any EA project be undertaken without a thorough assessment of enterprise-wide consequences. Make sure to include stakeholders representing various concerns in the EA process.

Analysis paralysis – As much as EA has a lot to do with research and analysis, it shouldn't become a hindrance to execution. Always remember that the ultimate goal of EA is to transition the enterprise to a future state.

Overemphasis on the current state – Never spend too much time or overstate the influence of the current state on achieving the future state. More time should be dedicated to articulating where the enterprise would like to go strategically.

Doing everything at once – Initially, there may be a tendency to tackle different issues at once. This is likely to result in nothing getting done. Try to prioritize the items that are key to the enterprise and will readily show the value of EA to your enterprise.

Summary

Chapter 1 introduced the idea of enterprise architecture being both a process and the product of that process. This chapter introduced how there are best practices to implement Enterprise Architecture. Furthermore, Enterprise Architecture can be considered a best practice in itself in relation to facilitating organizational change. The first seven chapters of this book addressed the latter.

This chapter has covered the best practices necessary to implement Enterprise Architecture effectively. Some best practices are nonnegotiable such as

- Hiring an experienced Chief Enterprise Architect who heads up the EA Program Management Office

- Securing stakeholder cooperation

- Developing a project charter

- Establishing the EA's value proposition from the onset

- Having an engaged project sponsor that you always keep in the loop

The prescribed steps have been developed through analyzing tangible experience and extensive research. However, it is important to factor in that you will most likely have to pick and choose the best practices to adopt, as well as adapt them to suit your enterprise's specific context. This chapter closes by highlighting common challenges and pitfalls that are faced during the EA process to enable you to avoid them ahead of time or identify them if they do arise.

CHAPTER 9

The Future Of Enterprise Architecture

Enterprise Architecture was initially introduced as a way of understanding and managing a business's technological assets. Businesses wanted a detailed picture of their system landscape and to know how its technological assets supported its business processes. Enterprise architects were required to paint this picture through modelling the existing architecture. Hence, Enterprise Architecture was mainly driven by the internal requirements and processes of a business. That has since changed dramatically as businesses have become more customer oriented.

Businesses are now driven by customer expectations to a much higher degree than before. EA has evolved accordingly, becoming a more strategic exercise in the sense that the future state of the business has to be designed to deliver maximum value to the customer. In this light, EA has now become a driver for digital transformation and innovation. Naturally, the role of the Enterprise Architect has also grown with Enterprise Architects now expected to introduce innovative ways of structuring the business's technological assets in a way that takes maximum advantage of the data available to the business.

© Sheunopa Chalmers Musukutwa 2022
S. C. Musukutwa, *SAP Enterprise Architecture*, https://doi.org/10.1007/978-1-4842-8575-6_9

Emerging technologies must be identified, evaluated, and mapped to the business's operating model to discover new opportunities. This must be done cautiously as not all new technologies are inherently suitable for the business purely because it is cutting edge. Hence, an Enterprise Architect requires an intimate knowledge of the business's operating models, stakeholder goals, and strategy to identify the most relevant technology for the business. In the past, an Enterprise Architect could get away with confining themselves to technical spaces, whereas the future Enterprise Architect must have a level of competence in business.

EA may initially start as a reactive exercise in an effort to adapt to changes in the business environment; however, the ultimate goal is to construct a proactive approach to dealing with pending change. For instance, Enterprise Architecture should result in the business having the agility to deal with unforeseen circumstances such as the COVID-19 pandemic. There should be a clear blueprint of your business and all of its moving parts in order to reliably etch out a way forward from any situation.

EA is not only about supporting strategy execution but also about assisting in the development of said strategies. The new technologies available to Enterprise Architects allow them to gain information about the business and its customers that can inform the development of new strategies. Such aspects will soon become prerequisites of any Enterprise Architecture program. In essence, Enterprise Architects will become internal management consultants responsible for end-to-end strategic technology integration.

The evolution of EA within the organization will not be a natural by-product of simply practicing EA within the organization but must be aggressively pursued. The maturity of the EA program will be reflected in the IT modernization efforts of the business as it adapts to a changing world. It is important to point out that since different parts of a business can be in different stages of modernization, the Enterprise Architect must support all of these transitional periods simultaneously.

Enterprise Architecture is still relatively young as a discipline. However, the increasing complexity faced by businesses globally is beginning to carve out a critical need for EA. With the introduction of new technologies occurring faster than ever, businesses need a structured way of adapting to change swiftly. This chapter explores how EA suits this need perfectly and what the future holds for Enterprise Architects.

New Challenges to Face

In a rapidly changing world, businesses are faced with new environmental realities. The COVID-19 pandemic of 2020 was the biggest trigger of these new realities. Businesses had to reimagine how they would run their organizations internally in terms of managing/supporting their staff and externally in terms of delivering services to their customers in the way most appealing to them. Even businesses that had plans for the greater adoption of online transactions had to accelerate their plans significantly. It was a reminder to most businesses that they cannot predict the future. Businesses should be agile enough to adapt to anything, and I mean anything. However, there are a few challenges standing in the way of most businesses.

The first challenge is EA itself. The new circumstances we face require EA to evolve to adequately tackle those new circumstances. This goes for businesses that have been actively practicing EA and those businesses looking to start practicing EA. Are frameworks such as the Zachman Framework first developed in 1987 still relevant? Granted, it has been updated over time, but it may be time to start with something from scratch – a completely new design instead of a redesign. Of course, how EA is implemented in the business will depend on the context of the business. Whatever the case may be, the EA program must be suited to the current climate.

The new realities the business faces result in the second challenge, which is dealing with increased complexity. With more businesses delivering services and managing their operations online, migrating to the cloud has taken center stage. Most organizations are likely to adopt a hybrid strategy by having some applications in the cloud and others on premise. This increased complexity begets more complexity such as the new security measures that have to be taken to secure technological assets. Some businesses may need to completely redesign their business processes and operating models to survive. Enterprise Architects will be tasked with navigating the business through the increased complexity introduced by these new realities.

Another challenge is that of the demand for a multicloud approach to serve the global market. Serving the global market means understanding the differing technology policies and legislature between countries. Particular cloud service providers may not operate in certain countries (China being a popular example), meaning the same business may have to engage different cloud service providers to serve markets in different countries. More commonly, we are more likely to see a multicloud approach taken in regard to a business continuity plan and having backups on different cloud service providers. Cybersecurity and data protection may face the same challenges when serving a global market. All of these factors introduce complexity that was nonexistent at the inception of EA. The architecture must account for all of this complexity and continue to support your customers seamlessly.

With the introduction of decentralized systems, working from home, and outsourcing of services, it will become more and more of a challenge to maintain an enterprise-wide view of the business. With stakeholder management being one of the keys to successfully implement an EA program, this becomes more difficult when all of the employees are not accessible in a central location. Furthermore, employees scattered across the globe will present language barriers and cultural differences that may make it difficult to communicate effectively. All of this may lead the

Enterprise Architect to only solely focusing on the parts of your business that they're comfortable with. Enterprise Architecture and Enterprise Architects will now have to be equipped with the skills required to build synergy across multiple cultures, decentralized locations, and differing economic environments.

The final challenge is that of skills. The skills required of an Enterprise Architect have increased dramatically. Historically, the Enterprise Architect's skillset would lean more toward IT, but with EA becoming more of a driver of strategy, it is imperative that the Enterprise Architect has a high level of business acumen. The modern-day Enterprise Architect is a combination of a solutions architect and a management consultant expected to comfortably lead a conversation with the CIO and the CFO equally. This kind of skillset will be difficult to find, with most people generally preferring to be specialist in one area or the other. Additionally, the Enterprise Architect must possess strong soft skills to facilitate stakeholder management. The EA skillset is broad and encompasses business domain knowledge, technologies, project management experiences, and organizational skills. This skillset will certainly be in short supply.

What to Expect?

Enterprise Architecture cannot predict the future. Nothing can. However, there can be an estimation of some scenarios that are likely to play out in the future and incorporate intelligence into our architecture that enables a proactive approach to change through providing strategic data-driven insights. This, combined with an agile architecture, will allow the organization to adapt to change quicker than most. This section will highlight some of the trends and expectations that will color the future.

An Expanded EA Scope

As has already been alluded to, the expectations of EA will increase considerably. What was mostly considered an IT discipline will truly become an enterprise-wide one. The importance of technology in driving business value is paramount in a digital world. EA will form the crux of an even greater alignment between business and IT. EA will incorporate activities that extract deeper insights into the business domain in an effort to identify technologies that not only align to business capabilities but also help identify emerging capabilities and opportunities. The business's architecture will incorporate intelligence that gathers insights that can inform strategy development. So, whereas EA was purely about strategy execution, its scope will now include strategy development. EA will be expected to deliver greater tangible business value.

Digital Transformation Will Be Nonnegotiable

Over the years, we've seen businesses lagging in the digital enablement of their business capabilities. The effects of the slow adoption of technology were not as pronounced as they are today. Most businesses could cling onto an old way of doing things as long as their customers had limited alternative options. That has changed dramatically as the global market has opened up. Businesses have become more customer-centric as customers now have access to a plethora of options at their fingertips. It is critical that the business implements the right technology to automate the business processes in delivering the best value to customers.

Technology is now more consequential to business. In the past, when online banking was down, it wasn't a disaster per se as most people still went to the bank physically. That has been turned upside down with most people drawn to the convenience of banking apps. A banking app being down for a weekend will cost the bank millions.

Migration to the Cloud

As more and more business transactions take place online, the migration to the cloud will be accelerated. With most organizations adopting a hybrid work-from-home/work-from-the-office approach as a norm, EA will have to evolve into a cloud-first discipline in order to be impactful.

Greater Cybersecurity Risks

In line with the expanded scope of EA, EA will become more considerate of cybersecurity risks in the development of architecture. It will no longer be about just optimizing IT capabilities but also about how to secure them. EA will create, examine, or determine the suitability of existing company cybersecurity policies, ensuring that recognized standards and best practices are implemented. Techniques such as zero-trust and threat hunting will be frequently used in addressing the possible security measures to be taken with increased working from home and outsourcing of services.

Reusability

Reusability is the ability to use an existing technological asset in the development of a new product or capability. More and more businesses are striving to develop as many reusable assets as possible to avoid the costs of building new products from scratch and to tackle any issues of technical debt. This approach fits in with the future-facing approach of EA as today's assets will be developed with future assets in mind. Solutions will not only serve the business in the present but the business will be able to integrate them in the long term. Reusability also delivers a level of consistency between components within the same architecture. This consistency may also reflect externally through delivering a consistent customer experience, for example, through having a consistent user interface over time.

Development Cycles Will Become Shorter and Shorter

DevOps is a mixture of cultural approaches, practices, and tools that increase a business's ability to deliver applications and services quickly.

DevOps is a cultural shift in the way enterprises operate. A consequence of adopting DevOps may mean having a central platform to develop, deploy, and test new functionalities within the context of best practices. DevOps is quickly becoming a norm as businesses compete to deliver value to customers at a faster rate. DevOps has become the key to creating and managing a consistent technology stack that is pivotal for supporting different development teams. As EA has traditionally been a long-term endeavor, it will have to adapt to this through agile EA. Agile EA embraces the principles and values of agile software development in its own right, and DevOps is complementary with agile software development. Instead of having one big bang approach to EA and digital transformation, continuous transformation will be the order of the day with a periodic updating of the desired future states of the business.

Enterprise Intelligence

Information architecture will be the main focus as businesses try to learn more and more about themselves and their customers. Predictive analytics, artificial intelligence, machine learning, and data science will play a critical role in educating your business. Data from predictive analysis may be leveraged in designing future state scenarios. Modelling of varying data sources will be important for EA to enable information-driven business models. It is important that this data is reliable because it will act as a fuel to any technological tool; the principle of "garbage in, garbage out" will still hold.

For instance, although SAP Enterprise Designer offers the functionality to draw your models from scratch, it's much more efficient to generate the model from data pulled automatically from the data sources within the enterprise.

The Future Enterprise Architect

Enterprise Architects are unique in the sense that they operate across the business in order to optimize how it runs within the context of its strategic goals. They require a high degree of innovative and creative thinking to assess business requirements, recommend technology, and model an architecture that enables applications, information sources, and technical infrastructure to achieve business objectives. This book is intended to be a practical guide to practicing Enterprise Architecture. Thus far, a lot of information has been put forward. Ultimately, what do all of these challenges and predictions of the future mean for the Enterprise Architect?

This section will empower the following individuals through expanding on what is expected of an Enterprise Architect going forward:

- The Enterprise Architect

- Those who will collaborate with the Enterprise Architect

- Those who will hire the Enterprise Architect

The role of the Enterprise Architect will go beyond modelling and IT standards but will see them become a vehicle for agility and innovation. This may seem daunting or overwhelming initially, but the Enterprise Architect now has more opportunities to contribute to the success of the business.

An enterprise architect will be expected to

- Deliver business value

- Have broad knowledge that covers all the domains

- Have researching skills

- Have an understanding of cloud strategies

- Utilize customer journey mapping

- Emphasize data-driven EA

- Have a knowledge of Enterprise Architecture methodologies

- Have an understanding of cybersecurity

Deliver Business Value

The word "architecture" gives the idea of producing copious amounts of documentation and models. In Chapter 8, we highlighted difficulties such as analysis paralysis that an Enterprise Architect can face as a result of doing too much planning and analysis. This is one of the areas agile EA intends to address. Enterprise Architects should focus on delivering business value by executing the first implementable unit of their plan no matter how small. It is these short sprints coupled with continuous feedback that will demonstrate the value of EA to stakeholders. Focus on business value and business outcomes by having a clear answer for "why" EA is being implemented by your business.

Broad Knowledge

As has been alluded to throughout this chapter, an Enterprise Architect will need a solid understanding of business and technology landscapes. The Enterprise Architect should be capable of acting in an advisory capacity for both domains. This uniquely positions them to have an enterprise-wide understanding of the potential impact of any strategic decisions, emerging business capabilities, or new technology. Normally, a technical business analyst would play the role of bridging business and IT but only within the context of a specific product or business capability. An Enterprise Architect bridges this gap for the entire business.

Researching

Innovation mainly comes from being well informed about the latest technology breakthroughs and applying creative thinking to develop a value-generating way to implement them within your business. Research drives the research and development (R&D) activities that a business carries out to innovate and introduce new products and services. Robust researching practices ensure that a business is well informed about its environment and its customers. This ultimately leads to a competitive advantage through the business being able to continuously adapt to its environment and customer demands.

An Enterprise Architect must have strong researching skills and must do so proactively rather than reactively in order to stay ahead of the curve. The desired future state of your business must never become fixed but must rather be continually updated in accordance with the latest relevant technological advancements. New technology trends are not to be implemented for the sake of it, but rather they must always be a means to an end such as the creation of new revenue streams. This implies that the research should go beyond technology trends but also include cutting-edge business ideas.

Cloud Strategies

Cloud computing and online transactions are here to stay, at least for now. Understanding cloud strategies, cloud migration strategies in particular, will be critical to an Enterprise Architect's skillset. For example, an Enterprise Architect should be able to advise whether the business should use a rehosting or refactoring strategy in their cloud migration. The former involves simply migrating the applications to the cloud as they are, whereas the latter involves adapting them to leverage cloud-specific features such as container-based environments.

Customer Journey Mapping

Previously, the business had to know the customer, and the Enterprise Architect had to know the business. Today, the Enterprise Architect must have an intimate knowledge of the customer journey and how it maps to business capabilities. This allows the Enterprise Architect to zero in on the IT capabilities and infrastructure that support the most revenue-generating business capabilities in the context of the customer journey. This allows for the optimization and improvement of the customer experience.

Enterprise Architecture Methodologies

It has been emphasized throughout this book that Enterprise Architecture methodologies should never be seen as a one-size-fits-all approach to Enterprise Architecture. However, Enterprise Architects should have enough knowledge of different Enterprise Architecture methodologies to use them as a starting point and customize them to suit their specific context. This customization should particularly focus on making the methodology adaptable to change.

Data-Driven EA

There are not many tangible and certifiable skills that an Enterprise Architect can possess beyond certification for an EA methodology such as TOGAF. However, with businesses becoming increasingly dependent on their data, a data science certification and a demonstrable competence in architecting information structures is of tremendous value. Today's businesses are formally and informally driven by data. Strategic decision making, operational decision making, and Enterprise Architecture itself require reliable data to produce results. Enterprise Architects should have the skills required to isolate relevant data and leverage it contextually.

Cybersecurity

The Enterprise Architect of the future must possess a working knowledge of cybersecurity concepts such as zero-trust. With a sizeable portion of modern architecture encompassing online platforms, cybersecurity will no longer be an afterthought or an exercise only undertaken after an incident has occurred. The Enterprise Architect must know all of the proactive cybersecurity measures that must be taken to protect the enterprise.

The Final Boss – Closing Thoughts on Stakeholder Management

As the saying goes, "the more things change, the more they seem to stay the same." Even with all of the changes, challenges, and Enterprise Architecture skills we have explored throughout this chapter, the most critical aspect of EA remains stakeholder management.

The increased complexity that businesses are facing means there will be increased uncertainty that is more often than not going to trigger anxiety among stakeholders. EA must ramp up its change management processes to ensure stakeholder buy-in. This was always a difficult activity, but this difficulty increases exponentially in the face of globalization and serving a global market. Successfully managing cost-cultural diversity becomes a key aspect of securing the support of stakeholders and delivering a successful EA program. The EA team should take every opportunity to engage with them about the required change through a "Let's try this, what do you think?" type of approach.

EA must not only seek to inform stakeholders but to inspire and motivate them toward change. This can be achieved through how the Enterprise Architect reacts to a need for change, even if they're not initially aware of how they will bring about that change. An EA should never be quick to say no but rather details the risks of any idea and the possible measures to mitigate it. This empowers stakeholders and helps them understand if it makes sense to proceed or not. Stakeholders must understand what EA does and how it positively impacts the work they do. Actively collaborating with stakeholders is nonnegotiable.

The Enterprise Architect must not collect data in a silo but must collaborate with the relevant stakeholders in their data collection efforts. This ensures that they can see things through the lens of the stakeholders and assess that from their own enterprise-wide view. There are many nuances that do not appear in a report or spreadsheet that you can gain when you engage stakeholders in their natural environment. Try to figure out how to collaborate and engage stakeholders in a way that suits them rather than yourself. Be careful to not overload stakeholders with information, but take your time to determine a pace that is comfortable for the stakeholders without compromising EA timelines.

The enterprise architect should always lead with business value. Stakeholders want to see results. One way of accomplishing this is by not reinventing the wheel. For instance, reimagine how the business leverages existing data and technological assets rather than starting afresh. Tap into the business's unexplored potential; look into the business first before exploring external solutions. The business may already have what it takes to transform the business in accordance with their business strategy.

Soft skills are of paramount importance in stakeholder engagement. Being present, showing empathy, consciously listening to stakeholders, and emotional intelligence, to mention a few, are some of the soft skills that will enable an Enterprise Architect to win over stakeholders. The modern EA will have to engage with board members and executive teams about the business implications of technology decisions. This process is significantly smoother through being relatable and likeable.

The Enterprise Architect must be able to use digestible business language to explain the potential impact of technological decisions. For instance, with globalization, using mergers and acquisitions is a viable strategy for increasing your global footprint through existing and established entities. The Enterprise Architect will be expected to explain how the existing systems of these entities are to be integrated or replaced in the context of business impact.

This can only be carried out effectively through practical business language and not the underlying technical jargon. At this level, Enterprise Architects can really influence change and investment decisions by articulating their business impact.

Lastly, the enterprise architect must be as proactive as possible and anticipate any questions before they're asked so that you can be prepared with the relevant answers. EA's currency within an organization is being able to provide actionable insights that stem from their multiperspective, enterprise-wide view of the business.

Summary

Enterprise Architecture enables you to understand the relationship between business outcomes, business strategy, and technology, which in turn empowers you to identify areas for improvement and sheds light on the changes required to optimize your enterprise. Enterprise architecture is future proof because it is a single source of truth, and your business will always need a single source of truth. Historically, this only referred to the IT standards, governance policies, and models found in the EA repository, but today it also refers to the data generated through intelligent architectures. EA can now facilitate strategy execution and also inform future strategy development.

Customer expectations will continue to drive innovation as they have been; Enterprise Architecture will provide the structure to the decision making and change implementation required to meet customer demands. This also means that the role of EA is now relevant to both the business and its customers. EA must produce end-to-end models that can generate valuable insights to drive digital transformation for both the business and its customers.

There are new challenges that EA must face mainly due to the increasing complexity introduced by businesses aiming to serve global markets. This often means the use of cutting-edge technology that the world is still trying to figure out; best practices for implementing that technology may not even exist yet. The modern Enterprise Architect must either upgrade an existing skillset or develop a new skillset entirely to lead the charge against these new challenges. Aspects such as cybersecurity and cloud migration strategies will be a focal point in establishing the enterprises of the future.

Lastly, the most critical element of Enterprise Architecture remains stakeholder management. You could have the greatest EA program, but it means nothing without stakeholder buy-in. EA will have to develop and implement approaches to stakeholder management that take account of culturally diverse and decentralized stakeholder groups.

Index

A

Alignment
    business capabilities, 30
    business case, 44–46
    business strategy, 27–30
    cultural alignment, 43
    definition, 25
    IT and business alignment, 38, 39, 42, 43
    IT and business processes, 35–37
    IT capabilities, 31, 32, 34
    typical alignment scenarios, 40, 41
Application architecture, 13
    application lists, 88
    applications and physical, 158
    architectural descriptions, 88
    business processes, 89
    components, 159, 162
    definition, 87
    diagrams, 88
    implementation, 158
    interface lists, 89
    matrices, 88
    modelling, 157
    objects, 159
    SAP EAD, 158

Application diagram, 88
Application lists, 88
Application matrices, 88
Applications, 159
Application services, 13, 90, 160, 162–164
Architectural building blocks, TRM, 90
Architecture areas, 161, 165
Architecture artifacts, 52, 57
Architecture Change Management, 64, 115–117
Architecture Development Method (ADM), 62, 63, 69, 94, 104, 110, 115, 118
Architecture domains, 12, 55–56, 71, 73, 91, 110, 158
Architectures
    baseline, 78, 79
    definition, 78
    layers, 78
    target, 79–81
Architecture vision
    business drivers, 69
    business environments, 74
    business operations, 75
    business strategy and goals, 71
    definition, 69

G, H

I, J, K

FSC
www.fsc.org
MIX
Papier | Fördert
gute Waldnutzung
FSC® C083411